Reflections on Multiculturalism

Reflections on Multiculturalism

Robert Eddy
Fayetteville State University
Editor

INTERCULTURAL PRESS, INC.

For information contact:
Intercultural Press, Inc.
P.O. Box 700
Yarmouth, Maine 04096 USA
207-846-5168

Book design and production: Patty J. Topel
Cover design and production: Patty J. Topel

Printed in the United States of America

00 99 98 97 96 1 2 3 4 5

Library of Congress Cataloging-in-Publication Data

Reflections on multiculturalism / Robert Eddy, editor.
p. cm.
Includes bibliographical references.
ISBN 1-877864-45-5
1. Minorities—United States. 2. Pluralism (Social sciences)—United States. 3. Multiculturalism—United States. 4. United States—Ethnic relations. 5. United States—Race relations. I. Eddy, Robert.
E184.A1R445 1996
306.4'0973—dc20 96-3043
CIP

Dedication

This book is dedicated to all the children of America. May you do a better job of creating a just society in the twenty-first century than your parents and grandparents did in the dark twentieth century.

Table of Contents

II

Multicultural Dialogicalism: Personal Examples

Foreword: The Politics of Multiculturalism and Education's Ultimate Demographic Challenge

Lloyd V. Hackley

If I had been hired as an educational consultant thirty years ago to design an educational system for the United States that would, after a short time, begin to preclude large numbers of Black, poor, or otherwise disadvantaged students from making substantial progress in education and, therefore, in mainstream America, there is no question in my mind that I would not have been able to design one better for that purpose than the system which has evolved over the last four decades.

At the heart of the politics of multiculturalism is the question of education—education for *all* people. American education has been cited over and over as having failed: failed in maintaining the country's competitiveness internationally; failed in accomplishing the basic goal of American education to mitigate for all Americans the obstacles to full participation in the society; failed in redefining and redistributing power according to the country's current realities; and failed in providing an environment which will enable all its students to achieve educationally to their maximum capability.

From the perspective of multiculturalism, it is this latter issue that should be of special concern because it not only affects all the others but profoundly affects the American social system as a whole. It can be stated fairly simply: children from parents who occupy high-status roles, whether they attend public or private institutions, move through our schools with access to course work, instruction, and expectations that prepare them for high-status roles; while lower-status children are not only placed disproportionately in course work with low-academic content, but also are subjected to behaviors which reinforce their lower status in the United States.

According to the 1990 Quality in Education for Minorities (QEM) Project:

- To reach parity in college attendance, 1.3 million additional minority students would have to enroll in college by the year 2000.
- To achieve parity in college graduation, the number of minority students attaining degrees would have to triple by the year 2000. They would have to quadruple in mathematics-based curricula.

Just as it is difficult to single out a particular group that can be held responsible for a problem of such magnitude, so too is it nearly impossible to cite a single cause. Nevertheless, certain social realities must be specified because of their great influence on the central issue—the gaps which remain in educational success between advantaged and disadvantaged children.

For nearly all of U.S. history, issues related to education have constituted the core of the dialogue between the Black community and mainstream America, as well as the dialogue among the various power wielders in the mainstream as they discussed Black people. From the early years the debate ranged over such questions as *whether* Blacks could be educated, what should be the *content* of that education, and *where* should Blacks be educated.

The greatest change in American schools in the past forty years has been the change in racial mix, or the massive change in the number of schools with much larger degrees of integration. In the landmark decision *Brown v. Board of Education*, the Supreme Court found that separate education was, by definition, unequal. *Brown* and national, state and local laws, statutes, consent decrees, and other court decisions have been directed at providing Blacks and other minorities with greater opportunities for higher-quality education—and a greater quantity of it—*so that these persons could become full participants in all aspects of American life* (emphasis and wording mine). But measurable change did not really begin in public schools until the mid-sixties.

In making the case for equality of educational opportunity, we argued for many years that all that was needed to eliminate educational disparities between Black students and White students were better schools, with improved facilities, modern resources, current textbooks, and better-trained teachers. Through civil rights successes, we desegregated educational institutions from kindergarten through the doctoral-granting universities. Access was increased during the sixties until now it is virtually total.

Just about the time that Black students were accepted into White schools in appreciable numbers, after 1965, the system across its entirety was lowering its educational standards for a variety of reasons, none of which legitimately had to do with the presence of Black students.

Most detrimentally, the objectives of *Brown* were not combined with the objectives of *Adams v. Richardson*, which was to higher education what *Brown* was to public schools. We did not produce comprehensive state plans that focused on outcomes rather than access and that defined the educational system as a continuous process from kindergarten to the doctorate; thus, we have not effectively reduced disparities in education or in the ends of education.

For minority students and students from the lower-status levels, formal education constitutes nearly the only source for gaining the knowledge and skills that graduates must have if they are to be considered educated. Thus, those who need the most from formal education suffer the greatest deprivation when the standards of education are set low or when there are two sets of standards, one low and one high, with both leading to graduation. Today, at long last, there is a legitimate demand for higher-quality education. I applaud all efforts to improve educational outcomes. However, keep in mind that students from lower socioeconomic levels suffered for at least two decades when standards were declining. Now, the instruments of higher-quality education are catching unprepared thousands of youngsters who through no fault of their own have not been prepared for greater rigor.

Most of the programs that have been designed to improve Black student involvement in higher education have been less than effective because they did not include plans designed to reduce the need for special programs. The programs, essentially, were concessions slated primarily to address the inadequacies of the current generation. A proper program would have required the K-16 system to implement educational initiatives to reduce the number of students requiring the concession. A clear case is found in remedial education and the *Adams* case.

Many of the charges and countercharges leveled, as the various sides waged their civil rights battles following the *Adams v. Richardson* decision, involved the issue of remedial education. Civil rights lawyers in the Department of Education charged that traditionally White institutions were using arbitrary and capriciously high admissions standards to deny Black students the opportunity to attend these institutions. Spokespersons for the traditionally White institutions argued that Black students' records did not reflect SAT, high school GPA, and class-rank profiles which indicated that they would succeed in these institutions.

The federal officials countered with two points relevant to this presentation. First, they stated that Black students could receive remedial education. Pointing out that the universities already were using remedial education for their admitted students, they complicated the issue by introducing the concept of compensatory education: that remedial education would compensate for all kinds of previous deprivations—economic and social as well as educational. Second, the case was made that Black students admitted to universities all over the country were achieving educational outcomes far exceeding levels that could be projected from test scores, both in undergraduate and graduate schools.

The civil rights attorneys were absolutely correct in their interpretation of the outcomes: in those early years following integration, Black students achieved higher performances than could be projected from their SAT or GRE scores, or from their grade point averages. The lawyers, however, did not quite understand the causes. Most Black students who enrolled in traditionally White institutions in those early years had been well grounded in basic courses in mathematics, science, and English; they had been educated in a nurturing, supportive environment; and they were the strongest, most highly motivated students that the Black community could produce. Certainly, equipment and resources provided the Black K-12 segment of the segregated education system did not match those provided the White segment; but Black students more than made up for gaps in content with higher motivation and a commitment "to make the community proud of me." Now, as indicated above, Black students' access to quality course work has declined.

The upshot is that the number of Black students requiring remediation in college has continued to increase to the current rate of some 50 to 60 percent, as compared with about 27 percent for White students ("College-Level Remedial Education in the Fall of 1989," 5).

Effective Academic Enhancement Programs (e.g., remediation), at the college level designed to make up for long years of inadequate K-12 education, require more than technical excellence, more than compassion, and more than the two combined. As stated above, schools are instruments of society and should educate children to participate fully in our national life. To do this, we must know where and how these students live and the effects society has on them individually and as members of communities.

From birth to eighteen years, children spend only about 10 percent of their time in school. By seventh grade, children will have spent 93 percent of their lives out of school. Even during school much of Black students' time is spent with other Black students in classes essentially made up of Blacks. Thus, more than 90 percent of their time is spent with Black persons and in Black neighborhoods with people who see the United States as virtually unchanged in its racism.

Thus, poor, Black disadvantaged students will have been exposed to conditions that predispose them to failure before they even get to school; so we have to help them develop the ability, confidence, and motivation to succeed academically. We must help them understand that intellectual success is attributable to hard work and that failure results from lack of effort.

In order for children to make the effort in education and to delay gratification long enough for the payoff that education promises, there must be strength at the following levels:

First, the children must have a well-developed sense of self-respect, self-worth, self-esteem, and individual dignity.

Second, children must have an abiding sense of the worth of their own people, and they must know that their classmates, teachers, and the greater society value their people as well.

Third, children must have respect for and loyalty to the United States. It takes about six or seven years in the social/education system for children to be able to interpret signals which "inform" them of the relatively lower status of certain people in this nation.

It has become clear that there are three ways that educational excellence can be withheld from children. They are:

1. legal separation of children into different school buildings and in different school "systems" with different "missions" and lower funding;
2. admitting students into the same buildings but placing them into classes with widely varying levels of content and expectations;
3. treating students even in the same class in ways that enhance learning in some and discourage learning in others.

This last point, teacher attitudes toward different children, deserves some additional discussion. According to the QEM Project, the number one myth in the United States pertaining to the education of minority youth is that many persons in education believe that "learning is due to innate abilities and minorities are simply less capable of educational excellence than Whites." Since "studies controlling for environmental factors repeatedly demonstrate that there is no basis in fact for this assumption"(37), the debilitating conditions are social, therefore, and can be controlled by communities and schools.

Studies also indicate that the most crucial variable in the teaching-learning equation in the school is the teacher and his or her attitude toward students. It is important, therefore, that staff development include more than technical emphases, e.g., pedagogical and content competence. Workshops must address the attitudinal paradigms that result in lower expectations for minority children and ineffective teaching methods.

Schools should show that staff development includes:

- Specific attention to structural barriers, behaviors, and prejudicial attitudes and values in school that impede student achievement.
- Institutional interventions that promote effective teaching, including assistance for faculty members who are less than effective with students culturally different from themselves.

Given the general condition of education, schools must be judged both by how well they improve the academic competence of the top quartile as well as by how effective they are in closing the gap between the best performers and those who are behind. The Education Commission of the States indicated that the number of minority students participating and succeeding in higher education is declining; the only question is whether the decline has already become a crisis or soon will be one. Clearly, we have not achieved educational equity.

Conclusion

Without doubt, schools have an enormous capacity to do great good for our children and, therefore, for our communities. At the same time they are staffed with human beings who come to the profession from all walks of life and with varying opinions about themselves and about children and students. Contrary to conventional wisdom, schools don't make communities; good communities, where there is concern for all the people, create and support good schools which educate all of our children. But the children at the bottom of this society and at the bottom of the academic chain are informed constantly by the world at large of their lower worth and of the lower worth of their people and culture. Children's natural intellectual drive will not thrive in such conditions. They will only continue academic pursuits if we let them know that the pursuits, the children themselves, and the end results are worthwhile. They will withdraw from the learning process if we don't, as whole communities, give children the support they need.

Although morality, humane considerations, and social justice should have impelled us prior to 1954 to give all our citizens the same consideration—in school and out—we know that it did not happen. In an economic sense, given our position in the world forty years ago—both in absolute terms and relative to the weaknesses of foreign countries—undereducated and demoralized Black children were no threat to the country. In other words, relegating the overwhelming number of Black Americans to the "other" side of town geographically and economically, except for menial jobs for the most part, was acceptable, since a sufficient number of persons from the majority culture could maintain the pace of development. Current data indicate that White males are leaving the workforce in record numbers. The quality of American education has dropped from second to seventh in the world economy, and nearly 90 percent of the workforce growth by the year 2000 will come from minorities, immigrants, and women. Enlightened self-interest ought to impel us now to change our ways.

Said another way, prior to 1954, people who did harm, who let harm happen, and who ignored the results of harm done, were only doing harm to Blacks and the Black community. Now, individuals who harm or who allow harm to happen, are hurting the United States. And it is not simply a matter of money; it is also a moral issue. What we have to do is close the gap between the *words* embodying our national principles and our *acts*—what we actually do—to make real the lofty principle of equality of opportunity. Even if we do it only for enlightened self-interest, it will require hard work by more of our citizens.

Ideally, schools are instruments that society uses to mitigate the effects of being a subordinate social group, including the effects of ethnicity, economics, gender, geography, and physical conditions. Cultural diversity must mean that we take all steps necessary to operate our schools in ways to close the gaps in educational attainment between the advantaged majority students and the disadvantaged minority students, who because of historic exclusion and current vestiges of that era are not benefiting from our socioeducational system to the extent that they will be enabled to participate fully in our national life.

A high level of shared education is essential to a free, democratic society. Ill-educated persons in our society are excluded from the chance to participate fully in our national life as well as from the material rewards that accompany competent performance. Nothing we do as a community is so directly connected to our idea of who and what we are, what we want to be, than what we accomplish in our public schools. The community, as broadly conceived, in direct cooperation with local, state, and federal governments, should take our own children and help them develop into healthy and productive adults, fully capable of assuming the roles and responsibilities necessary for maintaining an economically viable democratic society.

In the essays which follow you will see this basic theme emerge again and again. It may be in different guises, and from the perspective of different minority groups or focused on different domains of the human experience. But in the end, the ultimate challenge to American society lies in its demographics and the need to adapt our educational system to the realities that confront us. This book is dedicated, quite appropriately, to *all* the children of America.

Works Cited

"College-Level Remedial Education in the Fall of 1989," National Center for Education Statistics. *Survey Report.* U.S. Department of Education. May 1991.

"Education That Works: An Action Plan for the Education of Minorities," Report Summary. *Quality Education for Minorities Project.* Cambridge, MA., January 1990.

"Education That Works: An Action Plan for the Education of Minorities," *Quality Education for Minorities Project.* Cambridge, MA., January 1990.

Acknowledgments

I would like to thank my former English Department chairman, Dr. Booker T. Anthony, now Executive Assistant to Chancellor Willis B. McLeod, and my current chair, Dr. Ophelia M. Holmes, for teaching schedules that permitted me to work on this and other book projects. Their constant enabling support means a great deal to me.

The staff of Fayetteville State University Library were extremely helpful and generous. Eloise Cave and Vera Hooks enabled many searches to end fruitfully. My former FSU student and current colleague Preston Holder II wrote a program to transfer old and crucial files from CP/M to MS/DOS. Colleague and contributor Eric Hyman read and commented substantially on a number of versions of the introduction and afterword. Gladys M. Hill, English Department secretary, was a source of constant help and good cheer.

I want to thank the four external reviewers—the referees—who helped shape and focus this book. They assisted with the tough decisions regarding which essays should be omitted from this volume and which should shape its execution. The internal reviewers were critical readers, rigorous collaborators and genial partners. David S. Hoopes, Editor-in-Chief of Intercultural Press, supplied vital direction and relaxed pressure which helped keep the project moving forward. His criticism, encouragement and untiring assistance were decisive. Toby S. Frank, President of Intercultural Press, offered humor, dialogue and critical commentary which enriched the manuscript. Patty J. Topel, Production Manager, was careful and creative.

Finally, I want to thank my family. Mei-Lung suggested the idea and focus of this book. Her inspiration and tenacity were crucial. I thank our daughters Eileen and Serena, eight and five years old, for their patience, smiles, and their elemental questions about if and why books matter in an age of electronic and virtual realities.

Robert Eddy
1 June 1996

Introduction

Robert Eddy

Is the United States becoming more multicultural at the end of the twentieth century or less so? If by "multicultural" we are referring only to demographic changes, to the ethno-racial composition of the workforce and the general population, then the answer is yes. But if multiculturalism refers to a feeling of shared fate, to the need for changing identities, transforming our sense of self and of what it means to be an American, and of seeing what the United States looks like through the eyes of different groups, and especially if becoming more multicultural refers to the attempt to increase social and economic justice—then the answer is much less clear.

We in the United States are in the midst of ferocious debates, veritable culture wars, and a politics that demonstrates anything but multiple perspectives within groups. We find ourselves in the middle of fiercely competing monocultural claims. Each group seems to be hunkering down into its primary, traditional, or even its self-stereotypical identity. What are we to do? This book answers that we must dialogue across boundaries, work to make them permeable, and open ourselves to being changed by each other. Why should we open up to multiculturalism? Why, specifically, should Americans who don't want to or who feel it is not in their economic self-interest to embrace multiculturalism, do so? The writers in this book tell us convincingly that we should adopt multiculturalism so that we do not become monoculturally provincial in a global society, and so that we can survive in the twenty-first century as a democratizing force rather than a future Bosnia.

This book is divided into two sections. Part one is "Theories and Issues in Multiculturalism." Dennis Fischman's lead essay—"Getting It: Multiculturalism and the Politics of Understanding"—argues that "understanding is a precondition for politics." How can we increase understanding across group boundaries that are often completely closed to rational discussion and to the open give-and-take of a rich and mature emotional life? In his answer, which presents a more interactive theory of politics, Fischman analyzes three key themes in the Jewish tradition of dialogue: partnership in Creation, midrash, and exile.

The first theme—partnership in creation—emphasizes a world of relation between human and divine which replaced a human-less world of perfection. Relating this theme to our situation in late twentieth-century American society, Fischman writes that creation is not a one-time event; it continues. The partners in the Torah seek to perfect a creation that is never complete. Can the diverse ethnic and racial groups in the United States seek a similar goal of shared and continuing creation?

> If each group perceives itself as striving to create a better world in which its own needs, constructed by previous history, will finally be met, then it becomes possible for us to see where others are doing the same thing.... Reflecting on our own tasks, we can learn to recognize similar patterns of hope and struggle in other people's stories. With or without a belief in God, we can look at all social groups as partners in creation, and we can gain a glimmer of understanding out of which solidarity has at least a chance to grow.

There is a painful tentativeness even in Fischman's "glimmer" of hope that we can achieve partnership status in building a truly multicultural United States. Fischman's hopes for the future must be provisional because human history in the twentieth century is filled with slaughtered millions, in and outside of wars. Given the history of this century one cannot rationally be optimistic. But hope is not the same as optimism. Hope is based on a commitment to the democratic ideal that, in spite of the monstrous scale of death and suffering we have experienced, we can invent more human social structures and more humane selves.

The second theme in the Jewish tradition of dialogue is midrash. Midrash involves new interpretations of texts based on a historical sense of what has come before us, but with an openness to new readings. Midrash is a useful way of imagining our multicultural project because it involves the construction of bridges to face the inevitable collapses in communication that occur. "In midrash," Fischman writes, "we give meaning to a puzzling text by fitting it into a context that already defines our lives; in political dialogue, we use breakdowns in communication as spurs to discover the context of meaning that the *other* party inhabits." When breakdowns in communication happen we need to ask how "does the social world look to this person so that what they're doing, saying, or feeling makes sense?" Fischman reminds us that just "because we use empathy and insight to appreciate another's situation...that does not mean we have to give up our own point of view or stop thinking critically about the claims they make."

The third theme in the Jewish tradition of dialogue is exile. Just as the Jews were in exile in Egypt, we understand all groups as in exile when they are not accepted or understood and are not allowed or aided in fully participating in the social and economic fruits of a society. What must those of us who are committed to multiculturalism do in response to such conditions of exile? Fischman answers that "getting it"

> must mean learning to recognize the exile of others and committing ourselves to make the tasks that face each group into the central topic of public life. The dialogue between social groups must begin by focusing on the changes

> necessary to empower all of us to formulate our needs and state our claims. Above everything else, we need the chance to make sense, both to ourselves and to others.

How do we get to this political stage in American society where we open up to the exile of other groups? "What is needed," Fischman believes, "is nothing less than a transformation of politics from an arena of interest-group competition and elite planning to an occasion for dialogue, partnership, and return from exile for all of us wandering in the wilderness this day."

In the next essay, "Metaphor, Language, Games, Cultures," Eric Hyman presents a particularly lucid account of how metaphor and language condition our responses to other cultures in ways that most of us do not examine or explore. Indeed we look out at the world through the metaphor but do not see the metaphor itself or how it organizes our perceptions.

Hyman examines metaphors of verticality, which, without clearly saying so, imply value judgments: up is good and down is bad. Some of his examples: someone you don't like is *beneath* you; a person you respect is someone you *look up to.* Groups that are not mainstream are often called *subcultures.* Hyman notes that our concept of "normal and abnormal originates from a center-and-periphery metaphor, for statistical data center themselves around a *norm* and everything away from that is labeled *abnormal.*" We have the organic metaphor of the *body politic*, with examples like *healthy* or *moribund, marrying* other cultures, *fertilized* by outside influences. We also have the textile metaphor group. The United States is *unraveling*, some fear. We worry about the *fabric* of our culture.

If metaphors are so basic to our way of responding to the world and "potentially so pernicious because they express value judgments, usually *down-putting* value judgments, that are unacknowledged and thus not up for review, can anything be done about them?" Hyman's answer is that we have to observe the metaphor systems we ourselves use and those used by others and contest and dialogue about them. We can invent new metaphors that intend to be more democratic. Hyman does so with his extended metaphor for cultures, which he calls an "allegory of the gameroom." But his key point is that no metaphor system is value-neutral, including his gameroom allegory:

> Nor is this allegory value-free, any more than any other system of metaphor is value-free. It's a rhetoric designed to impose or smuggle in my values. By casting cultures and languages as games I might be reducing the premium put upon culture. I am doing this for the sake of diversity of outlook, flexibility of behavior, and tolerance for others, but those are still values, and they are values somewhat antithetical to the values of loyalty to one's group or subordination to one's heritage.

The third essay in the "Theories and Issues" section is Sam Girgus's "Shattered Images: From Consensus to Contention in Classic American Film." Girgus examines how the directors of such movie classics as *Giant* (1956), directed by George Stevens, Capra's *Mr. Smith Goes to Washington* (1939), and John Ford's *Drums along the Mohawk* (1939) reproduce an American landscape of particularly potent symbolism with powerful political implications. Girgus puts it this way: Thomas Paine's "belief in America as a Noah's Ark literally beginning history all over again, of the utopian notion of the American garden as an asylum for all the world's peoples manifests itself in the minds and works of these directors."

The films, according to Girgus, disguise "coercion and intimidation as apparent loyalty and unity." How do the films work to enforce supposedly democratic consensus?

> The endless space of the opening scene of *Giant* and the control and manipulation of time and space in *Mr. Smith Goes to Washington* indicate the absence of real alternatives in both the films and the culture to the consensus of the American idea. The lack of apparent or attractive systems outside the universalism and individualism, independence and community of the

> American idea engenders strong commitment to that ideology. The films present this ideology as an all-encompassing envelope providing shelter and comfort. Both films also suggest the power of that ideology to convince, cohere, celebrate, and control. While inclusion compels certain forms of sacrifice and transformation, the films often dissemble the cost of that transformation beneath the enthusiasm for participation. Indeed, the films strongly suggest a compulsion to use the American idea as a means for control and uniformity.

The Girgus chapter poses these central questions about classic American films while acknowledging the complex representation of ideology in the films: 1) "How do narrative and ideology function to position and represent difference and otherness?" 2) "Do the films silence difference?" 3) "Are minority vision and voice denied narrative authority in order to be incorporated within a dominant view?" 4) "Can we find traces of genuine dialogue and debate in which positions of consensus and dissensus engage and contradict each other for the purpose of achieving original expression?" Such questions need to be asked not just about classic cinema but, in the context of our national debate over multiculturalism, also about the other arts and the media, especially news reporting.

Victor Villanueva, Jr., in his essay "Literacy, Culture, and the Colonial Legacy" argues that minorities in the United States continue to experience the alienation of internal colonization. He modifies Mario Barrera's theoretical model of structural assimilation into three components:

1. The historical mode of entry into the dominant society by those seeking assimilation;
2. The number and distribution or concentration of those attempting to take part in the overall society; and
3. The racial and cultural characteristics of those seeking equity with the majority.

For number one—mode of entry—the key point is whether the

entry is voluntary or through wars, such as the American Indian wars or the Vietnam conflict. The second component that influences complete assimilation is concentration. Is the group large enough for the majority to feel threatened? The key point in component three involves racial and cultural stereotyping. Some groups are more welcomed (or less feared) than others.

Villanueva reminds us that the language and literacy debates in this country are crucial because they are really about education policy and social justice. He urges us to allow students their own voices because a "multicultural acceptance of voice would acknowledge different cultures' different ways with discourse, different rhetorics, thereby leaving the long colonial trail." An enlightened educational policy that intends to construct multicultural literacies in the classroom and beyond would best serve the

> needs of multiculturalism in exposing the degree to which the multicultural finds resistance in entrenched caricatures of difference, facile stereotypes, rather than in a bona fide politics of difference, in which there is a constant dialectical interplay between the things we all have in common and our cultural and historical differences.

The final essay in the "Theories and Issues" section of the book is W. Maurice Shipley's "The Mulatto in American Literature." Shipley begins by referring to Dennis Fischman's lead essay "Getting It" as a "tragic commentary on this country's failure to make substantive growth in understanding racial differences." Shipley is inclined to concur with Fischman that a group can "rightfully demand empathy the way it demands justice," but immediately adds that "empathy does not necessarily lead to 'justice.'"

Shipley contends that in a study of the mulatto in American literature and culture "one not only sees possibilities presented by intercultural melding but better understands much of what needs to be overcome." One stereotype that needs to be discarded is the image of the "tragic mulatto," who is "stranded, pathetically, between two races—a victim of racial limbo or doomed to a sad end." Langston Hughes captures the idea incisively in his poem "Cross":

> My old man died in a fine big house.
> My ma died in a shack.
> I wonder where I'm gonna die,
> Being neither white nor black?

On the other hand, there is the, at first sight, apparently positive image or "mythological stereotype" that suggests "that mixed blood somehow imbued one with mysterious and exotic qualities." But the mulatto as mysterious enigma, however exotic, remains strange and anomalous, an alien. In "I, Too," Langston Hughes invites all the exiles home:

> I, too, sing America
> ...
> Tomorrow,
> I'll be at the table
> ...
> They'll see how beautiful I am
> And be ashamed—
> I, too, am America.

In the second half of this book, "Multicultural Dialogicalism: Personal Examples," each of the five essays reveals different perspectives in answer to the question: What is a multicultural dialogue?

The first essay is Min-Zhan Lu's "Representing and Negotiating Differences in the Contact Zone." Lu's answer to the question of what is multicultural dialogicalism is embodied in her idea of the "contact zone," which she juxtaposes to "cultural tourism." Before we can find or enter the contact zone, we must recognize that most common approaches to achieving diversity amount to tourism because:

1. we perceive cultures as discrete and self-contained rather than interactive and constructed in relation to others;
2. we perceive ourselves as strictly inside one and outside the rest of the cultures;

3. we view our cultural identity as strictly determined by such markers as place of birth, nationality, skin color, or other biological features;
4. we view issues of race, class, and gender as separate rather than intersecting.

By comparison, the contact zone is an intercultural social space with an "emphasis on interaction, asymmetrical power relationships, and radical change." The contact zone pushes us

> to yield what we have, including our existing habits of thinking and using language, our existing knowledge of ourselves and others, and the privileges and authority we enjoy and take for granted. It invites us to cause waves, to ask how and why rather than just nodding politely to statements with which we agree or disagree. It also reminds us of the material consequences of our reading and writing. To represent and negotiate cultural differences from the perspective of a less powerful other can disperse and dissolve what had appeared to be solid ground, the foundation of one's life and dreams. It can bring confusion and pain, when every part of our sense of self is engaged or grappled with by voices reminding us of the forms of domination we perpetuate in the choices we make when envisioning who we are and who we aspire to be. Letting go of the glass partition on the tourist bus can bring material consequences—the possibility of becoming a stranger, an other, to those dear and close to oneself.

Are we willing to accept "confusion and pain" as the price for a multiculturally reconstructed society? Lu's moving answer is that we need actively to mobilize the "moral power of American democratic ideals—the principles of justice, equality and freedom—to pressure ourselves to overcome our fear of entering a contact zone where diverse cultures and people meet, clash, and grapple with one another." With an illuminating and generously self-debunking personal example of her "tour" of Harlem, Lu illustrates the differences between the fatuous safety of cultural tourism and the openness and uncertainty of the contact zone.

Next is James Helten's "The Accidental Culture: Disability and the Enduring Need for Closure." This chapter is based upon Helten's personal experience of leaving his "home culture" of able-bodied men and, through a devastating accident, being transported to the culture of the disabled. Helten's brief history of the culture of disability is connected to the dialogue he experienced and continues to live between his old able-bodied self and society and his newer identity as a member of the culture of disability. He reminds us that the

> fifty-year history of the commingling of people with diverse disabilities for social and political purposes, for athletic competition, recreation, and artistic endeavors, and for employment and other activities of mainstream society has resulted in the emergence of a "culture of disability" that seeks and deserves recognition and acceptance as a viable, contributing member of the new multicultural order.

What is distinctive in a multicultural setting about the culture of disability is that "unity within a culture is bolstered by the pride that members take in a readily identifiable common feature. There is no pride to be found in being born disabled or becoming disabled as a result of an accident." But as "disabled people must discover, and as people of all cultures must discover, closure in life is never achieved, yet we must continue to seek it. If we are to judge ourselves, we should do it on the character of our responses to the crises we face that define our humanity."

The third essay which presents a personal example of multicultural dialogues is Thomas Austenfeld's "No Sentimental Education: An Essay on Transatlantic Cultural Identity." Austenfeld is a German who came to the United States to study for a Ph.D. and now teaches college here. He argues in his essay that a "well-defined and reflected self-identity is essential for reasonable and productive discourse to occur in society."

The personal experience he focuses on as a German born in 1960 is a presentation he made to two different American audiences about his coming to terms with the Nazi nightmare of 1933-45. The first audience, fairly homogeneous, consisted of "white, Midwestern college students." Austenfeld ended his presentation recalling how a visit to Auschwitz made when he was a student left him "speechless for days." The reaction of the audience to the entire presentation "evinced the standard shock that any of us would feel in the presence of human suffering," but still the audience responded to the event "essentially as an academic learning experience."

The second audience was "composed of students from Chicago's South Side and from the Deep South—at a historically black college in a southern state." In this group a "small but articulate minority of both Palestinian and African-American students challenged me on my portrayal of the Jews as victims." These students "equated Israel's treatment of the occupied territories with the Nazi's persecution of the Jews."

Austenfeld's first reaction to the second audience was that his "naive belief that victimized groups—Jews in Nazi Germany, Blacks in the United States—feel solidarity with each other was no longer justified." Upon reflection, he developed three proposals to support intercultural negotiations: through the culture of debate, polyglot education, and the fostering of tolerance and tact.

The first, the culture of debate, "would take place among equals whose intention is not necessarily to convince one another, but whose commonality lies in their willingness to learn about different perspectives on the same question." How would this proposal apply to his two audiences?

> If I brought the two student groups with whom I discussed German history into communication with each other, they would probably learn more about each other than about the topic at hand. As the "teacher" fades into the background, the process of intercultural debate has begun. At least for a time, participants in the debate would see the world from a different

> angle of vision and would consider respecting that alternative."

The second proposal is that an intercultural society should promote polyglot education—which is often interpreted as learning a foreign language. But competency in other languages "may only be the first step toward intercultural competence." What is also needed is the "ability to move between social classes or religious and ethnic groups and to act as 'translator.'"

The third proposal is the fostering of tolerance and tact. Austenfeld is only too aware that "'tolerance' and 'tact' may sound like easy subterfuges," but he adds that "in the practical, everyday world of multicultural encounters, 'tolerance' and 'tact' take on meaning at a surprising rate of speed. I would invite readers to test my proposals in their own lives."

In her essay, "Chinese in America or Chinese-Americans: Building Multicultural Landscapes and Literacies," An Lan Jang asks a question that is relevant for all minority Americans who see themselves as African American, Asian American, Hispanic American, etc., and who possess what could be considered dual loyalties: "What does it *mean* to be a Chinese in the United States, or a Chinese American?"

> The differences between being a Chinese in America or a Chinese American are profound. Did I see myself as a sojourner who would one day return to China? Did I want something in the United States that I would, after obtaining, "take home to China"? Or, would I put down roots and become a Chinese American? Finally I had to admit that my life was tied to the political possibilities I envisioned in a (potentially) multicultural democracy in the United States. I really have become a Chinese American. I have dual loyalty: to Chinese culture and its possible permutations and to the political entity, the United States, and to its possible political transformations.

What, for Jang, connects her dual identity is the Confucian concept of *jen*. She explains *jen* this way: the "literal meaning of *jen* is 'two people' or 'double persons.' The connotation of *jen* is that one should treat others as oneself" and, Jang adds, that "personal actions should not be built on selfish or individual motivation. The well-being of the family or group must always be put first."

After describing multicultural landscapes and literacies, Jang ends her essay by referring to mixed race, multilingual children: "We adults have created the monoculturalism of ethnic cleansing and surplus populations, while...children...are creating our best hope for a multicultural future."

The final essay which presents a personal example of multicultural dialogicalism is a literal dialogue by Solange de Azambuja Lira, from Brazil, and her American husband, Arnold Gordenstein. The title they chose is "The 'Other' before Me: A Bicultural Dialogue." This conversation, and in part confrontation, is a remarkably frank and insightful exchange. Part of its strength comes from their contextualizing the conversation with reference to Tzvetan Todorov's *The Conquest of America: The Question of the Other*.

The following portion of their dialogue concludes with three crucial questions about multiculturalism which we all need to contemplate.

Solange: Your background predisposed you to multiculturalism as much as mine did. It was no accident that you found a foreign mate. You probably even saw me as an oppressed minority like yourself. I only wonder what I saw in you through the "otherness" screen.

Arnold: You saw a high-tech caribou who won the horn-bashing contest. Remember him? To tell the truth, I find the inaccuracies in these perceptions of one another even more tantalizing and disturbing than the direct hits. For instance, compared to me, you were never a downtrodden minority. I might have regarded you as a downtrodden minority but you were from the ruling class in Brazil. You had 95 percent of the population below you, economically and politically. I mentioned the symbolism of us before, the Capulet and Montague of us. I think we saw a lot of symbolism in each other at first, and that's a lot of what the "other" is.

Solange: So you're saying that we may have come together because we both seriously misread one another? Is that what multiculturalism is in for? A series of mistakes, reading the symbols for the realities?

Theories and Issues in Multiculturalism

Chapter 1

Getting It: Multiculturalism and the Politics of Understanding

Dennis Fischman

It was the problem that had too many names.

In 1991, as the U.S. Senate was about to permit an undistinguished black Reagan lower court appointee to fill the Supreme Court seat that Justice Thurgood Marshall had reluctantly left vacant, a black Republican woman stepped forward to accuse the nominee of open, repeated, and gross acts of sexual harassment. The senators, all male, seemed confused on how to proceed. They had passed laws against sexual harassment, but as the hearings went on, it became obvious they had little idea what the term actually meant, or what sexual harassment looked and sounded like in practice. Faced with an unprecedented situation, the senators reacted as if they were a court of law, trying to weigh the evidence in a criminal case. The Judiciary Committee hearings on the Thomas nomination rapidly turned into the trial of Anita Hill.[1]

Yet, for the millions of Americans who watched or listened and debated the meaning of events in offices and coffee shops across the country, the issues extended far beyond either the conduct of Thomas or the credibility of Hill. What was at stake in the hearings was something both deeper and more personal than a Supreme Court nomination, and yet something that varied across the lines of gender and race. As the controversy went on, it became ever more clear that different portions of American society understood the problem they were discussing in different and sometimes diametrically opposite ways.

For many African Americans, both men and women, the prospect of seeing a black man "lynched" (in the evocative term Thomas used) for crimes with which white men are rarely even charged was apparently just too much. The accusations against Thomas, echoing ancient slanders from the days of slavery, became an indictment of African-American men as a group.[2] Polls showed African-American support for Thomas running high, and National Public Radio interviewed male and female customers at black-owned restaurants who said they wished Anita Hill would just shut up. But many women, of all races, saw the spectacle of fourteen rich, powerful white men trying to shake the testimony of a woman who had risked her reputation and her career in order to lay a charge of injustice before them as a badge of women's degradation. The fact that both the woman and the man who allegedly harassed her were black seemed irrelevant; it just appeared to show that sexism knows no color.

Most painful for these women (many of whom would not call themselves feminists) were the questions even supposedly liberal senators asked Hill over and over: "Why did you put up with the sexual harassment? If it was as bad as you say, why didn't you just leave?" Across the country, a single phrase leapt to the lips of female reporters, members of Congress, and viewers alike: "They just don't get it." Their realization was in its own way as stunning as "The personal is political" (the key insight of the resurgent feminist movement of the 1960s) had been twenty-five years ago.[3] For with the recognition that the political leaders (and much of the public) of the United States do not begin to understand the lives of anyone who is black or female comes the dawning awareness that once again, the boundaries of politics need to be challenged and, eventually, changed.

In the 1990s, the phrase "They just don't get it" has become a rallying cry. To the conventional language of public debate, however, it is brand new.[4] What kind of grievance are people expressing when this exclamation rises to their lips? As citizens of a liberal society, Americans know how to respond to certain kinds of claims: that rights have been denied, power abused, privileges taken, or injustice done. We have theory that can define these wrongs. We have institutions whose job it is to right them. But what do we make of a complaint that the situation of a particular group (for instance, the situation of black men or black women) has not been understood? When a claim like this is lodged with the court of public appeal, it implies that we, the people, have a responsibility to become aware of one another's condition in life. Can a group rightfully demand empathy the way it demands justice? Is understanding a political issue?[5]

I want to answer these questions, simply, yes. Understanding may be an unfamiliar political good. Calculations of who gets what, when, and how may usually leave it out. For people trying to take advantage of democratic procedures to end a history of exclusion, however, having oneself understood is vital. Within the "new social movements" aimed at ending racism, sexism, and homophobia, lack of understanding from the public at large is blamed for making oppression invisible, or silencing the expression of a group's cherished identity.[6] Blocked from effective political participation by the constant need to educate an uncomprehending public, women, people of color, gay men and lesbians, and other historically excluded groups find themselves governed by officials who cannot represent them due to inability to conceive the problems for which they are seeking solutions.

When members of a less powerful group tell members of a more powerful one, "You just don't get it," they are saying, in effect: "You don't know us. You don't share our predicament in this society, and you lack the good will or the imagination to put yourselves in our place. When you try to talk about our problems, you sound both unfeeling and stupid. How can you judge us? You don't recognize our needs when we shout them at you. How can we trust you with power over our lives? Why should we?"

These are questions of legitimacy, questions basic to political life. Unless those who ask them can be satisfied with the answers, government by consent of the governed is impossible. Let me make the claim even stronger. Without a climate of mutual understanding among all major social groups, a society can have order, even government, but not politics. Politics, at its best, involves the recognition of others as real as we are, people who can surprise us and, sometimes, win us over. "Not getting it" means being unaware of the people among whom one lives except as shadows of oneself—what Marx once called "the other-beings of thought"[7]—or as helps or hindrances to one's own interests. Without a commitment to understand one another, we cannot be citizens, people who strive together to create a society that meets the needs of all.

For if any of us "just don't get" what it means to be a different kind of person in our society, then we will not include them—or they will not include us—in this society's idea of a good human life. Someone's urgent human needs will be excluded from discussion. Silently, power will be exercised before questions of power can even be brought up. The responsibility to understand one another comes before specific theories of rights, obligations, freedom, justice, authority, and legitimacy, and before the institutions we create to secure these ends. For without mutual understanding, we cannot trust one another to seek out political principles and practices that will allow each of us to fulfill his or her human needs—nor to change our politics if they fail to serve us all.

If there is any field of study we expect to prepare us for political life, it is political science. In the United States, however, after World War II, political science became wedded to a positivist view of knowledge and a behaviorist approach to the study of politics that together made questions about citizenship, human needs, and the failures of liberal political systems impossible to ask.[8] As a result, by the late 1960s, political theory (as a distinct and critical approach to the study of politics) experienced a renaissance.[9] Both older and younger scholars rejoiced at the chance, in the face of fundamental social problems, to consider fundamental issues of politics once again.

The promise of political theory has not been kept. Within the discipline of political science today, the few theorists whom political scientists generally read are the ones who seek out universal principles of justice and try to spell out the rights and obligations of individuals in a way that any rational person would accept. The model for this endeavor is John Rawls's *A Theory of Justice*, in which the author asks us to imagine we do not know to what sex, race, or class we belong and then to choose the principles of justice we could accept even if we found ourselves among the least privileged members of society.[10] Liberal theories like Rawls's have noble intentions, but they ask us to believe the unbelievable. They insist that people can suspend their own experience and interests in order to choose neutral principles. More crucially, liberal theories assume that more privileged people can choose principles of justice that will satisfy the needs of less privileged groups—without finding out what, exactly, those needs are.

Among political theorists, the critics of the dominant liberal paradigm far outnumber its defenders.[11] Most theorists try instead to elucidate the common understandings that bind us as a community, or to unmask the relations of power hidden in capitalism, the family, patriarchy, or political discourse—or, they dissect the sinews of discipline that give the body politic its shape.[12] Each of these approaches has enriched the terms of political discourse in academic life, as well as giving social critics the legitimacy they need to win jobs at universities (which is no small feat). The triumphs of political theory have, however, remained academic. Instead of transforming the study of politics, let alone political life, political theory has increasingly become a "separate table" at the corners of the discipline.[13]

If I am right that understanding is a precondition for politics, however, dissenting political theorists could presently offer only limited aid to the least powerful people in our society, no matter how much influence they exercised, because their theories do not commit them to "getting it." Of course, liberals, communitarians, Marxists, and postmodernists can all feel sympathy for oppressed people as fellow human beings. Far be it from me to deny that. Oppressed groups suffer, however, as groups, from particular conditions, the full weight of which it is difficult to appreciate from an external perspective. Without understanding the experience of the group in question, theorists of justice can only help the least powerful by accident, as their "universal" theories now and then happen to touch the circumstances of the group in need.

The liberal demand that theory be universal and meaningful to everybody may even prevent particular claims from being considered politically significant at all. (Sexual harassment, the crime with which Hill charged Thomas, was considered humorous only a decade ago because men could not imagine themselves as its victims.) Similarly, communitarian theorists tend to assume that "we" share common understandings and to overlook the conflicted process of forging those understandings out of disparate experiences.[14] Critical theorists detect, in one situation after another, the strategies of power with which they are already acquainted, but nothing in their theories expressly commits them to learning about other, less familiar oppressions. We can and must do better than that.

In this chapter, then, I want to propose to political theorists a new goal for the theory we do: namely, "getting it." To argue the full case that we should make mutual understanding the hallmark of our theory would require a wide-ranging investigation, and I shall not attempt it here. Instead, I am going to assume that many theorists share a frustration with the increasingly isolated way we go about trying to understand political life, but don't yet know what else to do. For readers who are searching for an alternative, I want to give a sketch of how a more interactive kind of theory might work, what the process might look like in practice.

But there is a problem with my attempt to do this. If understanding one another is the challenge we face in order to create a better politics (which some would call a politics of multiculturalism), then I would have to be arrogant indeed to think I have already surmounted it: that I already understand you well enough to show you how to "get it." To move from incomprehension to empathy, you have to discover the key to which your ear is already tuned and practice listening in the range you now find too hard to hear. That will be a different training for each individual. Even if I knew you well enough to be your guide, what about the next reader, whose needs differ from yours? The nature of writing for a public audience makes it impossible to give a one-size-fits-all description of how we come to understand our neighbors.

So, instead, in the following pages, I will begin by setting out some of the principles of a politics of understanding. Then, I will illustrate them by explaining how I use the resources of my own tradition to help me understand myself and others and the different voices in which we speak. At the heart of the Jewish tradition, we find a relation of dialogue, an I-Thou relationship between humanity and God for the purpose of perfecting the creation of the world. This model of dialogue, if we use our imaginations a bit, can suggest ways political theorists can bring mutual understanding and joint action into our practice of political theory. I will explore the implications of three important themes of that tradition—partnership in Creation, midrash, and exile—for the pursuit of a multicultural political community. Finally, I will sketch some connections between "getting it" and building political coalitions.

I

> Any normative claims about society make assumptions about the nature of society, often only implicitly. Normative judgments of justice are about something, and without a social ontology we do not know what they are about.
>
> —Iris Marion Young[15]

The liberal tradition that has dominated modern political thought ever since the Enlightenment has popularized certain "assumptions about the nature of society" that make "getting it" a difficult thing for us to do. As liberal theorists have imagined it, society is merely an assortment of varied, distinct individuals. Neither the society as a whole nor any social group to which the individual may belong is real in itself, only as an extension of the will of its individual members. Individuals exist prior to societies and to social groups. Each person is fully formed, if not at birth, then at least by the time he—and it is a "he," in classical liberalism—becomes politically active: it is a terrible breach of liberal etiquette to ask how taking part in the hubbub of political life may reshape citizens in their very selves. For preserving oneself and one's own self-interests are considered the only rational motives for individuals to take part in society at all. Society, then, is a mass of desirous individuals pursuing either the natural needs of their bodies or the arbitrary preferences of their personal whims, in opposition to all other individuals, who compete with one another for the use of limited resources.[16]

With this view of social life, it is no wonder that up until recently, liberal political scientists have treated the demand to be understood as unnecessary, undesirable, unhelpful, or impossible to fulfill. Why invest any energy in the attempt to understand others when, at bottom, we are all the same? I seek what I need and what I want; so do you. What more is there to say? If I try to grasp why you want what you do, moreover, I run the risk of losing sight of my own interests, which are necessarily my first concern. "To be totally understanding makes one very indulgent," wrote Madame de Stael.[17] That indulgence is a luxury few can afford in a world of competition to acquire, possess, and control. It takes great presumption on your part to demand that I grant you such an advantage.

As a discrete individual, I will not voluntarily concede anything unless you can make it in my self-interest to do so—but I will respond even to abstract principles of justice if I am convinced I stand to gain overall by so doing. Therefore, you do not really need me to understand your situation. You need the power to insure I will find it worthwhile to meet your demands, and if I do that, what I understand or misunderstand is no concern of yours. So why should we bother to discuss it? In fact, we cannot really put ourselves in the place of others, anyway. As individuals, we can never know what it is like to be anybody else. I can observe you from the outside and try to discover what makes you act the way you do—in other words, look for causes—but I cannot understand your reasons for acting. The unique impulse that makes each of us what we are finally remains a mystery. "Getting it," according to this view, is an illusion.

If we follow this well-worn track in modern political theory, we shall get nowhere. In order to take "getting it" seriously, we will need a whole different notion of social reality than the one which has captivated liberal thinkers. What assumptions can we make about society that will allow us to give priority to the task of understanding one another?

To begin with, we have to think of society, not as a congeries of individuals, but as a set of people in relationships structured by the particular set of social groups that at this moment comprise society. According to Iris Marion Young:

> A social group is a collective of people who have affinity with one another because of a set of practices or way of life; they differentiate themselves from or are differentiated by at least one other group according to these cultural forms.[18]

Not every group in society meets this definition. "Nazis, socialists, feminists, Christian Democrats, and anti-abortionists are ideological groups" who share political beliefs; "recipients of acid rain caused by Ohio smokestacks" form an interest group of people who are similarly situated with respect to a particular phenomenon.[19] Neither of the two is what we mean here by a social group. Social groups, in the sense Young intends, might include women, gay men, lesbians, African Americans, Asian Americans, Jews, working-class people, or poor people, as well as whites, middle-class people, Christians, and men. The list is obviously incomplete, and the groups listed overlap considerably, but they share one defining characteristic.

Social groups differ from interest groups or ideological factions precisely because, although they are socially constructed themselves, they create and reproduce larger-than-individual differences among the inhabitants of a society. This construction of differences is a second factor to include among our assumptions about social life in order to give importance to "getting it." When we are trying to understand the problems that members of another social group face, we have to treat those differences as real. For the members of that group, they are real: not all in their heads, not to be wished away, not arbitrary, but theirs—and ineluctably tied to their group identity.

For instance, there is currently a real divergence between the outlook of many black men and black women in this society, as not only Anita Hill but many African American women writers have brought to public attention.[20] This difference, we can assume, is not biological but historical in its origins. It is surely no accident that in a community which has often phrased its struggle for social justice as "regaining our manhood," men should feel entitled to claim the full support of the community and women should feel obliged to give it.[21] Nor is it surprising that black women, many of whom provide for families in which they are the single parent or the sole wage earner (or both), should resist making further sacrifices to support their precious men—especially since as black women, they earn far less than black men, let alone white men, either compared to men who do the same job or considering black women as a class.[22]

The point here is that what it means to belong to a particular group, like black men or black women, varies both with that group's material status and with how that status is interpreted. The differences between the two groups cannot be reduced to arbitrary preferences, and yet they are not essential traits, either. Rather, the "set of practices" and "way of life" that each group follows, both together and apart, shape their worldviews and bestow their identities upon them. Because the group partially defines the self, members of any social group have a personal stake in whatever affects the group as a whole. What is at stake for them is what we grasp when, at last, we "get it."

Already, with these conceptions, we have moved far from the liberal view of social life. To establish the importance of "getting it," however, we need to know more than that social groups are different and shape the identities of their members in ways that matter. Social groups also interact, and their interaction has profound consequences for individuals. There are no timeless truths about being Jewish, gay, upper class, or female, to pick out a few of the many things to be. The meaning of each of these identities stems from the opportunities, expectations, limitations, and burdens assigned by their respective positions on the social map.[23] But neither is identity voluntary. People do not create their social status by themselves. The privileges of belonging to the upper class spring from past social interactions in which they acquired their wealth and power and from present relations of deference to property and official position. The burdens of being black in the United States are also socially constructed: they involve both structural discrimination and racist attitudes that pervade our communal life.

To know the problems of another person, we need to understand the situation of their race, ethnic group, sex, class, sexual orientation, or culture, because that situation often creates their predicament. For any of us actually to solve problems imposed by the way society treats the social group to which we belong, we need to have our injuries recognized as legitimate grievances that the polity ought to redress. That recognition will be withheld unless, when men look at women's troubles, or whites at the troubles of blacks, Hispanics, and American Indians, they "get it."

Why did I not write, in that last sentence, "When women look at men's troubles," or "When blacks look at the troubles of whites"? Certainly not because being male or white, or both, guarantees a happy life. The understanding we seek to make central to politics must be mutual understanding. Indeed, since social groups do define one another, investigating any group outside of its relations with all the others necessarily distorts our perspective. Yet if we do seek to validate the intuition that political theory must promote "getting it," then we must also recognize that some social groups have more power than others to define social reality. Some have enough power to subject others to "the denial of one's own voice through the imposition of an external, alien standard for the interpretation and judgment of one's thoughts, actions, and being" that Shane Phelan calls "oppression."[24]

Hence, although the expression "You just don't get it" springs out of a specific failure to understand in the Anita Hill case, it always implies a broader critique. We don't "get it" because we live in a society that refuses to recognize the needs people feel as members of a social group. We don't "get it" because we ignore the unequal chances that different groups can make their own needs the object of legitimate political claims. Above all, when we don't "get it," it is because we don't have to: because no one has the power to force us to confront the problems other groups face. A commitment to "getting it" means advocating a standard of social justice far beyond anything currently accepted in American politics.

II

It is one thing to describe a conception of social life that authorizes us to make mutual understanding the cornerstone of our politics. It is quite another to put that idea into practice. Although every political theorist makes background assumptions about the nature of society, and some assumptions impede the work of understanding one another while others promote that goal, still, no philosophy standing alone can force us to recognize when we are still not "getting it." Our commitment to principles of understanding does not guarantee that we will know when or how to apply them. To practice mutual understanding, we need more than good will: we must be able to discern the issues at stake in a particular dispute for a particular group with which we are not affiliated. In order to do that, we require a lot of specific information about people in different social groups with whom we live, as well as repeated and habitual experience in recognizing their needs and responding to them. "Getting it" is not a skill or a definable set of techniques. It involves judgment and sensitivity; in the long run, it means instilling into ourselves a certain kind of character.

Liberal theory, of course, promises to guide collective action and justify authority without reference to the character of the citizens. But liberal theorists are lucky: they possess a master narrative that does half the work of virtue. They can wrap this tale around any situation like mapmakers projecting a grid over new terrain. Once upon a time, they say, we lived together in the state of nature. Conflict and uncertainty threatened our peaceful existence. So, we came together under a social contract that dictates the terms of coexistence for people in civil society. The social contract solves the problems that beset us in our natural state, and as long as we follow its rules of reason, we shall live happily ever after.

As characters in this story, we know how to act our parts: we mind our own business until conflicts arise, then refer to the rights society was formed to protect—and protect them. To most Americans, this story makes sense at the gut level. In fact, the story is what makes sense of nearly everything else we do, so that many of the gains that oppressed groups have made in this country were explained in terms of the liberal narrative and legitimated by its moral force.

But if we are convinced that these gains are not enough, it will take more than just a new set of concepts to move our neighbors to start "getting it." A deeply ingrained narrative which helps to organize the stories of our individual lives can only be displaced by other, equally compelling narratives. In place of the saga of the social contract, I suggest we start telling a tale more adapted to our need for training in the process of understanding each other. That is the tale of the dialogue between God and humanity, as recounted in the Hebrew Bible, or Torah.[25] By appreciating the main themes of that story and by transposing them onto the dialogue between social groups in the United States, we can give the project of "getting it" the credibility and the urgency it deserves.

When we open the Torah and let ourselves into the biblical narrative, we immediately find ourselves in a world of relation. Look, for instance, at the actions of God at the start of the book of Genesis. Why would a perfect, all-powerful being want to create the world, anyway? The rabbis who gave the first recorded commentary on the Torah came up with an intriguing answer to this question. God created the world because, they said, God was lonely. No rugged individualist, this deity. In all the glory of heaven, God still needs company. We may smile at the innocence of this explanation, but as long as we remember it, it has its effect. The more we tell each other this story about Creation, the more we come to think of living in relation as a natural and fulfilling condition.

Human beings are literally constituted in relation to God. It is not only that when the first human being awakes, God is there, waiting. We owe our existence to God's desires and to the act of creation that makes mud into man. The story of the creation of woman from one side of man echoes the declaration, "Let us make man in our image, after our likeness," we hear from God only a little earlier in the account. God's likeness (not mere resemblance, but kinship of purpose) includes woman as well as man, even if patriarchal interpretations have sometimes glossed over this point.[26] The Creation story comes in two different versions in the first two chapters of Genesis, but both tell us that we exist in a fashion shaped by our relation with others.

Yet this shaping occurs in more than one direction. By creating the world, the God of the Torah becomes dependent on us, creatures that we are. If God is lonely and makes human beings out of a longing to be understood, the limits of our ability to imagine God restrict the fulfillment of that desire. We respond only to the God we can comprehend; unknowingly, we dictate in this world how God can be.

Furthermore, human beings as portrayed in the Torah have free will. We act from our own purposes, putting God's chances of enjoying a satisfying relationship at the mercy of our fickle human whims. In this world, God becomes something different from the Infinite and Omnipotent. God becomes one of the characters in the story. Despite the vast inequalities of power between us, both the human and the divine partners in this cosmic odd couple need one another and set the conditions for the other's identity.

Now, if we could think of our social world along the lines of the world of the Torah, it would be a good start toward accepting the responsibility of "getting it." None of the social groups among whom we live has created any of the others, certainly, but short of that, we are intertwined in almost every relationship one can imagine. Some groups historically have lived in the same neighborhoods and fought over turf, like Irish and Italians, or blacks and Koreans. Some groups have migrated to this country because the United States invaded theirs, like the peoples of Indochina and Central America, or as refugees from other invaders (whose kin settled in the United States as well). Some groups relate to one another because people they include in their community identify equally with other social groups: working-class Jews, Native American lesbians, black bourgeoisie.

Most significantly, some social groups are bound to one another by a shared creation story. We can trace the emergence of groups called "homosexuals" and "heterosexuals," and find it is the same process that defines them.[27] We can go back in history and follow the rise of racial ideology that made black and white people separate races in this country while establishing three races, Black, White, and Coloured, in South Africa, groups which exist only in relation to one another. It would be absurd to imagine capitalists without wage workers, and it would be equally absurd to look for either group much earlier than the Industrial Revolution that made them the predominant classes in Western societies. We may not have wished for each other's company, as God does in the biblical story, but like God and the human race, the different social groups in the United States are stuck with one another, our destinies bound together.

What is the content of the relationships we are discussing? Are these only abstract connections, or do social groups have a basis for real dialogue? Again, let us turn to the Torah for a model of a dialogical relation. In the biblical story, God and humanity are partners in the ongoing process of creating the world. Creation was not a one-time event, nor is it ever complete. Although God looked on everything God made and "saw that it was good," human beings are responsible to invest everything with significance, to lift nature out of mere objectivity and give it a part in the story of God's encounter with humanity. To borrow a phrase from Martin Buber, we are partners with God for the purpose of hallowing the world.

Being in dialogue with God, therefore, makes it incumbent upon us to act. If nothing else, we must continually make the effort to find out to the best of our abilities what God wants in the situation. By engaging in dialogue with God, we already take a step toward hallowing the world, because we take our unpremeditated actions and consciously give them direction. Our most mundane actions become special to us when we do them "for the sake of heaven"; eating and drinking, for instance, done with a holy intention, become sacred acts.

Yet partnership in creation demands more than a higher level of awareness of what we are doing already. The biblical story gives us countless examples in which human beings are called upon to change their social institutions in order to promote God's purposes in the world. Often, we are called to act in explicitly moral terms:

> ...to deal thy bread to the hungry, And that thou bring the poor that are cast out to thy house....When thou seest the naked, that thou cover him, And that thou hide not thyself from thine own flesh...(Isaiah 58:7).

Not only are we to eat our food with the right intention, in other words, but as we do so, we have to make sure others can eat as well. The Torah impresses on us by both precept and example that we must go out and look for chances to make the world better—that anything less than that is letting our divine partner down.

This model of dialogue—as a partnership in creating a good world—has much to teach us about the dialogue between social groups. God and humanity need to understand each other because they have a task to do together, hallowing the world. Their task is not optional: it comes from the same creation process that brought these characters and their setting together. Social groups are also constituted by the historical processes that unified them at a given time, and groups, too, have tasks to accomplish that they cannot do alone. The immediate task is to preserve the group's cultural identity, and this is one reason each group wants to be understood—because they need the other groups' recognition. Entering into dialogue is itself a way of making a better world. Having others hear about your problems and "get it" is already a kind of liberation.

In most cases, however, simply being heard is not enough. Many social groups face the additional task of trying to change the world so they will no longer be exploited, dominated, or stunted by social institutions. In the Bible, humanity (and particularly the Jews) accept the task of hallowing the world from the hands of God. The tasks that oppressed groups in the United States have to bear have been assigned by more profane powers: each group strives to undo the injuries of its social position. The fight against racism is an existential condition for people of color, as the struggle against homophobia is for lesbians and gay men and the resistance to anti-Semitism is for Jews.

The oppression of each group is specific, and so the job each has to accomplish in order to participate equally in politics is specific, too. Oppressed groups cannot make do with a common political analysis, nor can they oppose a common enemy, without erasing the differences whose impact on their lives is real and vital.

Paradoxically, the possibility for coalition arises from within the differences. If each group perceives itself as striving to create a better world in which its own needs, constructed by previous history, will finally be met, then it becomes possible for us to see where others are doing the same thing. Jews can recognize the needs of African Americans without making them identical to their own needs; straight women can see how they could face the oppression that lesbians do without denying the specificity of their identity. Reflecting on our own tasks, we can learn to recognize similar patterns of hope and struggle in other people's stories. With or without a belief in God, we can look at all social groups as partners in creation, and we can gain a glimmer of understanding out of which solidarity has at least a chance to grow.

III

Sometimes when we think we are on the verge of "getting it," other people shock us by telling us angrily that we still don't understand. Tensions may run high and tempers may flare between people who believe they have made an honest effort to put themselves in another's place and people who find themselves misunderstood—still—by those they had hoped would be their allies. Partly, the bad feelings that result from a failure of understanding stem from unrealistic expectations about how easily we can comprehend each other if we try. The situation in which we expect to understand another's communication but don't is familiar to interpreters of texts; indeed, a whole science of hermeneutics developed in the Western world out of the desire to understand the Bible despite the difficulties of doing so.[28]

In the Jewish tradition, a special hermeneutical style developed before European thinkers took up the problem. This is midrash, the searching interrogation of texts that continues the Jewish dialogue with God beyond the era of revelation and prophecy. As "partnership in creation" provides us with a more useful set of assumptions about social life than the liberal theory of the social contract, so, too, does midrash give us an especially good model for the process of coming to understand the situation of other social groups.

Why is understanding the Torah a difficult thing to do? In part, because in the Jewish tradition, reading the biblical story is not a literary exercise: it is a way of recommitting ourselves to our relationship with God and the task we have to accomplish together. Understanding the Torah means constructing a sense of what God wants from us and how it is appropriate to respond. Any number of things can make that process problematic. The gap between a divine point of view (even circumscribed by the limits of God's role as Creator) and a human standpoint is vast, keeping us always uncertain whether or not we have truly bridged it. We have also to cross a historical divide between the time the Torah was written and today. How did our ancestors relate to God differently than we do? How would they record their experiences differently, and how does their written record translate into events we have known? How would God speak to them to make them understand, and what words should we put into God's mouth to mean the same to us today? Finally, as always, we have to apply the lessons we learn from the Torah to the concrete situations we encounter in our own lives.

It would be impossible to do all this were it not for the stories of relation with God which guide the interpretive process. What a text can mean to a reader is nearly infinite, but what the Torah can mean to traditional Jewish readers has to fit with and make sense in light of the story about partnership in creation we have already heard. Midrash is the process in the Jewish tradition by which new meanings are invented. As Max Kadushin describes it, in midrash, readers approach the text with a few well-defined "value-concepts" in mind: not values, but recurring themes to search for in the text. These preoccupations arise from the standpoint of a partner in dialogue with God, seeking to understand God's ways and God's expectations of us; from the point of view of the rabbinic tradition, the text becomes meaningful when and only when it addresses these concerns.[29] But since the Torah is presumed to be wholly meaningful, the job of the reader is to find ways to imbue every word, every letter, even the spaces between the letters with significance for our task of hallowing the world.

Through midrash, for instance, rabbinic readers took the phrase "You shall not seethe a kid in its mother's milk" (Exodus 23:19) and derived a commandment to eat dairy foods separate from meat dishes, one aspect of the dietary laws known as *kashrut*. Keeping kosher made attention to the partnership with God an integral part of the daily routine. Another example: in the text of the Torah, injunctions to care for strangers and do justice to the oppressed are regularly capped with the reminder, "You were strangers in the land of Egypt" (for instance, Exodus 22:20). So, the rabbis scoured the Egypt story, looking at just how the Jews were treated there, in order to know what to avoid doing to the foreigners and the vulnerable among them.

In midrash, the reader approaches the text actively looking for problems, gaps, discrepancies, contradictions, all the ways in which the Torah does not make sense at first glance, given the situation of the reader. To make a midrash, the reader must use imagination, creativity, even a degree of daring in order to bring the problematic passage back into the world of the dialogue. A successful midrash will make the text speak to the project around which the partnership with God is organized. Although the goal is serious, the attitude of midrash is playful. It can afford to be. For as long as the interpretation restores the sense that the Torah narrative goes on giving shape to our lives, questions of method and even of consistency are not troubling, and the reading has the authority of something "told to Moses at Sinai."[30]

Now, we would not want to encourage members of one social group to assert this kind of authority when they try to interpret the situation of others. A spurious sense of expertise is part of the oppression against which people are protesting when they say, "You just don't get it." Making midrash is like striving to understand another person, however, in terms of the obstacles to be overcome. Group differences add to the ineliminable differences of individual personality to make "getting it" a never-ending process, like trying to know the mind of God. Furthermore, because social groups have long histories together, every time a member of any other group interacts with an African American, for instance, they bring the history of Africans in the United States and the specific relation between their group (Southern white women, let us say, or Jewish men) and African Americans into the relation. They may be aware of their history to different degrees, having different stakes in understanding it, and what they do remember, they may interpret in conflicting ways.[31] Even if they share a common story about who they are and what they're doing here, reaching agreement on any kind of joint action may be difficult, even impossible. The tasks we need to accomplish sit close to our sense of self, but the imperatives that drive and help constitute each social group may or may not harmonize. No god commanded the social construction of race, gender, ethnicity, and so on in the United States, and there are no guarantees that what we ourselves have created can be peaceably resolved.

What we cannot carry over from midrash into political life is the reassurance that comes with a continuous tradition. What we can borrow is, first, a sense that the project of understanding one another is necessary, urgent, and inescapable, and second, a happy realization that when we fail to make sense of one another, it is an opportunity to extend and deepen our acquaintance. In midrash, we give meaning to a puzzling text by fitting it into a context that already defines our lives; in political dialogue, we use breakdowns in communication as spurs to discover the context of meaning that the *other* party inhabits.

When we find we're just not "getting it," instead of giving way to frustration, we can ask ourselves: How does the social world look to this person so that what they're doing, saying, or feeling makes sense? What kind of dialogue are they involved in, and what kind of world do they need to create? When we strive to suspend our own conception of reality and view social issues from someone else's standpoint, so that we truly "get it," the willing suspension of disbelief that authorizes midrashic interpretations is a habit of mind we need. Just because we use empathy and insight to appreciate another's situation, of course, does not mean we have to give up our own point of view or stop thinking critically about the claims they make.

In fact, by "getting it," we have the chance to become better critical thinkers than before, since the point of view we start out with ceases to seem the natural or the only way to think. By doing midrash on the divergence between the standpoints of various social groups among whom we live, we understand our own social location and what it implies.

IV

The idea that "getting it" about others may lead us to a better understanding of ourselves sounds wonderful at first, but it should give us pause. A better understanding of ourselves: if we don't already know who we are and what we need, how can we tell others? If we can fail to understand ourselves, then presumably others can misunderstand themselves, too. In that case, what hope do we have of grasping their situation? It is all very well and good to enter into dialogue with other social groups, to listen to their story, and even to reconstruct it for ourselves, along midrashic lines—as long as they can confirm our interpretation or object to it and make us work a little harder. But what if, because of the oppressive social system we live in, some social groups are not in a position to help us "get it"? Suppose something about the social structure or the dominant culture makes it next to impossible for a group to formulate its predicament in a coherent way, or to present it to other groups in a manner that will be taken seriously. How could we hope to achieve an inclusive society, a legitimate government, a satisfying political life?

The story that models this dilemma in the Jewish tradition is the story of exile. As I have described it in my book *Political Discourse in Exile*, for Jews to live in exile is to live in a culture that demands we think, speak, act, and feel in ways that contradict a specifically Jewish sense of identity.[32] "How shall I sing the Lord's song in a strange land?" the Babylonian exiles lamented. Certain ways of hallowing the world cannot be done outside the promised land; others apply only to a self-governing people, not one scattered among the nations. The diaspora deprives us of the conditions we need to hallow the world without relieving us of the responsibility to do so.

Exile means not being able to carry out our task except in sporadic and disjointed ways. It means the story we live is broken off in the middle, the dialogue between God and ourselves is interrupted, our partnership is on the rocks, and we have lost our compass in daily life and have to navigate all alone. The biblical stories that resound with the theme of exile—the expulsion from Eden, the confusion of languages at Babel, the destruction of the Temple—all emphasize that the loss of meaning is a tragedy. Reading these stories, we can hardly bear it. Exile demands we put all our force into finding a way to return.

We begin to return at the moment we recognize that we are in exile, that the contradictions we experience are not character flaws but effects of our contradictory place in American society. A group in exile cannot become whole by rejecting either aspect of its identity, neither its particular features nor those it shares with other groups. Modernizers among Eastern European Jewry used to urge their people, "Be a Jew at home and a man [sic] in the street." But this is impossible. We are both Jews and citizens: we can never be simply one or the other. Western society has shaped all the social groups it has touched, and partly for our benefit. We would not give it up if we could. Yet in this society, we are not at home as long as the tasks we need to accomplish are considered private matters, and the galling part is that this sense of strangeness is not an issue we can raise with others without putting the blame on ourselves.

I think Anita Hill must have felt this way, as if to state her needs were to describe herself as a strange, abnormal type of person, and making a claim was automatically giving others the grounds to deny it. She had ceased to pass. By lodging a charge of sexual harassment against Thomas, she had placed herself with the women instead of the Republicans, with the women instead of the elite, with the women, even, instead of the African American community. She could not be both. She would not be allowed to be both. But being a woman makes one a private figure, with only personal problems, nothing that carries weight in public deliberation, nothing to say in politics.[33] She is included in political life despite herself because of the sexist oppression that dogs her steps, but she is excluded by the definition of sexism as a women's problem. Anita Hill, it seems, is in exile.

"Getting it " about our neighbors, we come to see, cannot mean understanding their group identity as if it were a simple, unproblematic thing. Part of what constitutes a social group is the way that it lives in exile in a society that attaches no importance to group differences. "Getting it" must mean learning to recognize the exile of others and committing ourselves to make the tasks that face each group into the central topic of public life. The dialogue between social groups must begin by focusing on the changes necessary to empower all of us to formulate our needs and state our claims. Above anything else, we need the chance to make sense, both to ourselves and to others.

It is entirely conceivable that a group may make demands at first that its members will not consider equally important later, as they gain more trust in the responsiveness of others. That should not be held against them. We are in dialogue with people, not abstract positions: we should expect them to change. Because people do change, political dialogue requires a high level of attention to each other—not constant, but always alert to the signs that further adjustments may be about to take place. Political dialogue therefore means giving up the typical American assumption that we only need to pay attention to politics intermittently, when problems crop up, and that once those problems are quickly solved, we can plug up our ears again. That is not how to sustain a relationship, let alone a country.

To be realistic, though, the kind of attunement to one another we are talking about here is something many people have a hard time maintaining (if they see the need for it) even in their intimate relationships. Men have begun to pay attention to women's needs, for instance, not because of the cultural values espoused by feminism, but mainly because their earning power has declined, and they have become more dependent on their wives' income. Middle-class women have also slightly increased their ability to live independently from men, and they have made this gain through their own efforts, not through the good will of men. If it takes a shift in bargaining power to get men to attend to the women with whom they are intimate, then we must assume that it will take even more to make members of one social group listen to members of another with whom they do not share a home. We should not base our hopes for a politics of mutual understanding on anyone's good intentions. We can insure to every social group the right to demand that others "get it" only by changing the existing relations of power within our social institutions.

It is not difficult to imagine ways of reorganizing government that would give oppressed social groups a greater voice in public affairs than they have now. We could replace the single-member district, majority election system by which we choose our legislators with some form of proportional representation. We could move from "one person, one vote" to cumulative voting, in which a person can either vote for as many candidates as there are positions to fill or cast all his or her votes for a single candidate who best represents that person's interests. Perhaps the key to increasing the influence of these groups is not who fills the seats but, once they are filled, how the lawmakers reach decisions. We could require that certain bills in Congress need not only a simple majority but a majority of the women, or of the Hispanic people, or of the Congressional Black Caucus, to pass.[34]

There are two enormous problems with an approach like this, however. One is the difficulty of achieving the reforms. The only justification we could give for them is the urgency of the need for mutual understanding—but if people agreed to that, then the reforms themselves might be unnecessary! Even more crushing, however, is the realization that giving social groups a larger say in the political arena might not help matters a bit as long as they face the same old constraints on what can legitimately be considered a matter of public debate.[35] Many African American women appeared before the Senate Judiciary Committee during the hearings on the Thomas nomination, but all combined, they could not make the senators understand her situation nor even concede the need to try.

What is needed is not merely more influence for social groups whose wishes have in the past carried little weight. The power to make one's needs known is not a commodity that can be parceled out more or less evenly among groups in society.[36] What is needed is nothing less than a transformation of politics from an arena of interest-group competition and elite planning to an occasion for dialogue, partnership, and return from exile for all of us wandering in the wilderness this day.

I do not know of any force in American political life that is capable of bringing about this transformation—and yet it is urgent. Therefore, I end this paper on a frankly utopian note. My hope for the future springs from two sources. One is the faith that coalition work among diverse social groups seeking a multicultural society will necessarily require new norms of mutual respect and new practices of coming to terms with one another. Bernice Johnson Reagon is undoubtedly right to caution against mistaking one's coalition for one's home.[37] Political work with people who have different needs than I do will often place mutual understanding lower on the agenda than developing a shared program. The two are not unrelated, however, and at the very least, multicultural coalitions provide places and times when people can get together in the name of their differences. With luck, this kind of political work will create a "movement culture" that will affect the larger culture as well.

The other straw to which I cling is the possibility, slight as it may be, that writing essays like this, using theory to break down the walls that theory has always buttressed instead, will open free spaces for the imagination. Perhaps the time is right for a few pregnant words like "getting it" to ripen into thought, and thought into action, and for learning to lead to a better life. Anita Hill did not know, when she chose to testify, what effect her words would produce. None of us do. We must speak up for a better society nonetheless.

---

[1] The trial goes on. In *The Real Anita Hill* (New York: Free Press, 1993), David Brock accuses Hill of various personal and political crimes, including not really being a Republican. For refutations of Brock's poor documentation and sloppy reasoning, see Jane Mayer and Jill Abramson, "The Surreal Anita Hill," *New Yorker* (24 May 1993), 90-96.

[2] On the myth of the Black man as rapist, see Angela Davis, *Women, Culture, and Politics* (New York: Random House, 1989), 42-44, and various essays in Toni Morrison, ed., *Race-ing Justice, En-gendering Power* (New York: Pantheon, 1992).

[3] The slogan "The personal is political" has been persistently misunderstood by men and women who never participated in the women's liberation movement. "Feminists did say that the personal was political, but they meant that private relations between the sexes reflected public divisions of power, that putatively private events, like wife beating, were public concerns. They didn't mean that getting to know yourself was sufficient political action. Consciousness raising was supposed to inspire activism." Wendy Kaminer, *I'm Dysfunctional, You're Dysfunctional: The Recovery Movement and Other Self-Help Fashions* (Reading, MA: Addison-Wesley Publishing, 1992), 31.

[4] True, Ted Koppel had used a similar phrase during his 1988 election year interview with Michael Dukakis. Koppel tried to get Dukakis to respond to the "demon liberal" image the Bush campaign had foisted on the Democrat through relentless negative advertising. Dukakis insisted that the voters cared about competence, not ideology, and would see through the attacks. Koppel sighed and said, "You just don't get it, do you?" The phrase became a reminder of Dukakis's supposed insensitivity to what Americans really cared about.

[5] That understanding and caring for one another are part of our ethical obligations is now commonly accepted among moral theorists influenced by the work of Carol Gilligan. For Gilligan's own writing, see the bibliography in Joan C. Tronto, "Beyond Gender Difference to a Theory of Care," *Signs* 12(4), 1987: 644-63, and also Carol Gilligan, Jane Victoria Ward, and Jill McLean Taylor, with Betty Bardige, *Mapping the Moral Domain: A Contribution of Women's Thinking to Psychological Theory and Education* (Cambridge: Harvard University Press, 1988), and Carol Gilligan, Nona P. Lyons, and Trudy J. Hammer, *Making Connections: The Relational World of Adolescent Girls at Emma Willard School* (Cambridge: Harvard University Press, 1990). See also Nel Noddings, *Caring* (Berkeley: University of California Press, 1984), and Sara Ruddick, *Maternal Thinking: Toward a Politics of Peace* (Boston: Beacon Press, 1989). As Tronto points out, however, whether an ethic of care produces a better political order is a separate question. (See her recent *Moral Boundaries: A Political Argument for an Ethic of Care* [New York: Routledge, 1993].) Gilligan's work is notoriously insensitive to differences of race, class, and ethnicity, a defect only partly repaired by Mary Field Belenky, Blythe Clinchy, Nancy Goldberger, and Jill Tarule, *Women's Ways of Knowing: The Development of Self, Voice, and Mind* (New York: Basic Books, 1986).

[6] Iris Marion Young, *Justice and the Politics of Difference* (Princeton: Princeton University Press, 1990) 58-61. See also Adrienne Rich's essay "Disloyal to Civilization" in *On Lies, Secrets and Silence* (New York: W. W. Norton, 1979), 276-310.

[7] Jerrold Seigel, *Marx's Fate: The Shape of a Life* (Princeton: Princeton University Press, 1978), 134.

[8] See David M. Ricci, *The Tragedy of Political Science: Politics, Scholarship, and Democracy* (New Haven: Yale University Press, 1984), and J. Peter Euben, "Political Science and Political Silence," in *Power and Community: Dissenting Essays in Political Science*, ed. Philip Green and Sanford Levinson (New York: Random House, 1970), 3-58.

[9] Sheldon S. Wolin, "Political Theory as a Vocation," *American Political Science Review* 63 (1969), 1062-82.

[10] John Rawls, *A Theory of Justice* (Cambridge: Harvard University Press, 1971). For an application of Rawls's methods in a feminist context, see Susan Moller Okin, *Justice, Gender, and the Family* (New York: Basic Books, 1989).

[11] One of the most influential critiques of Rawls can be found in Michael J. Sandel, *Liberalism and the Limits of Justice* (Cambridge: Cambridge University Press, 1982).

[12] I am not thinking of particular authors here but of whole movements: interpretation as influenced by Aristotle, Hegel, Wittgenstein, and Clifford Geertz, critical theory stemming from Marx and Freud, and genealogy as developed by Nietzsche and Michel Foucault.

[13] Gabriel A. Almond, "Separate Tables: Schools and Sects in Political Science," *PS* 21, no. 4 (Fall 1988), 828-42.

[14] Okin raises this objection against communitarian theory on behalf of women, but she argues that women, as a group, share so many of the same interests and needs that she can speak for women even on an international scale (Susan Moller Okin, "Gender Inequality and Cultural Differences," *Political Theory* 22:1 [February 1994], 5-24). For a spirited rejoinder, see Jane Flax, "Race and Gender as Barriers to and Possibilities for Communities," paper presented to the Western Political Science Association, Albuquerque, NM, March 12, 1994.

[15] Young, *Justice and the Politics of Difference* , 25.

[16] See C. B. MacPherson, *The Political Theory of Possessive Individualism* (Oxford: Clarendon Press, 1962).

[17] Madame de Stael, *Corinne*, cited in *The Oxford Dictionary of Quotations*, 3d ed. (Oxford: Oxford University Press, 1979), 517.

[18] Young, 186.

[19] Young has recently proposed that Sartre's concept of the *series* fits this kind of adventitious collective. See Iris Marion Young, "Gender as Seriality: Thinking about Women as a Social Collective," *Signs* 19, no. 3 (Spring 1994), 713-38.

[20] For instance, Alice Walker, *The Color Purple* (New York: Washington Square Press, 1982); Gloria Naylor, *The Women of Brewster Place* (New York: Penguin, 1988); Toni Morrison, *The Bluest Eye* (New York: Washington Square Press, 1970); Terry McMillan, *Waiting to Exhale* (New York: Pocket Books, 1993).

[21] One need only listen to any of the speeches of Louis Farrakhan to tell that the rhetoric of manhood is alive and well in the American black community.

[22] See National Committee on Pay Equity, "The Wage Gap: Myths and Facts," in Paula Rothenberg, ed., *Racism and Sexism* (New York: St. Martin's Press, 1988), 69-72.

[23] For the concept of the social map, see Peter Berger, *Invitation to Sociology* (Garden City, NY: Doubleday, 1965).

[24] Shane Phelan, *Identity Politics: Lesbian Feminism and the Limits of Community* (Philadelphia: Temple University Press, 1989), 16.

[25] I use the Hebrew term here not merely because it is most familiar to me, but because the Christian term "Old Testament" reeks of contempt for Judaism. *Testament* means covenant, and "Old Testament" reflects the Christian doctrine that God's relationship with the Jewish people was done away with and replaced by a new covenant through Jesus. Even the Pope has now repudiated this doctrine. For the various implications of "Torah," see Dennis Fischman, *Political Discourse in Exile: Karl Marx and the Jewish Question* (Amherst, MA: University of Massachusetts Press, 1991), 46-47.

[26] See Arthur I. Waskow, *Godwrestling* (New York: Schocken Books, 1978), chapter 5 and throughout. Judaism is a complex weaving of many different strands of thought, some more inclusive of women, some less. Many Jewish feminists have tried to make new patterns by weaving in their own threads, through the process of interpretation called "midrash" that is described in part III of this chapter, into the fabric of the old. The result is not only a more inclusive Jewish community but a stronger one, besides. "Feminism... demands an understanding of Torah that begins by acknowledging the injustice of Torah and then goes on to create a Torah that is whole." Judith Plaskow, *Standing Again at Sinai* (San Francisco: HarperCollins, 1991), 9.

[27] David F. Greenberg, *The Construction of Homosexuality* (Chicago: University of Chicago Press, 1988).

[28] See Paul Ricoeur, *Essays on Biblical Interpretation*, ed. Lewis S. Mudge (Philadelphia: Fortress Press, 1980). For an interpretation of the meaning of the exegetical tradition, see also Hans-Georg Gadamer, *Philosophical Hermeneutics*, trans. David E. Linge (Berkeley: University of California Press, 1977).

[29] Max Kadushin, *The Rabbinic Mind*, 2d ed. (New York: Blaisdell Publishing, 1965).

[30] All interpretations of the Torah deemed worthy of consideration are assumed to have been revealed to Moses in an "oral Torah" that accompanied the written revelation at Sinai. See D. Fischman, *Political Discourse*, 80.

[31] See James Baldwin and Nikki Giovanni, *A Dialogue* (Philadelphia: Lippincott, 1973), and W.E.B. Du Bois, *The Souls of Black Folks* (New York: Dodd, Mead, 1961 [1903]), ch. 9.

[32] D. Fischman, *Political Discourse*, ch. 5.

[33] Jean Bethke Elshtain, *Public Man, Private Woman: Women in Social and Political Thought* (Princeton: Princeton University Press, 1981).

[34] Lani Guinier, *The Tyranny of the Majority: Fundamental Fairness in Representative Democracy* (New York: Free Press, 1994).

[35] This is a major theme of Tronto, *Moral Boundaries*.

[36] See Young, *Justice and the Politics of Difference*, ch. 1.

[37] Bernice Johnson Reagon, "Coalition Politics: Turning the Century," in *Home Girls: A Black Feminist Anthology*, ed. Barbara Smith (New York: Kitchen Table Press, 1983).

Chapter 2

Metaphor, Language, Games, Cultures

Eric Hyman

Usually when we think of "culture" we think in broad terms of broad entities. We may think of a culture as coextensive with a nation-state (American culture, Mexican culture, Chinese culture) or a large geographic region (European culture, Western civilization, the Indian subcontinent) or a religion (Christian, Islamic, Buddhist, animist) or an ethnic group (white, African American, Irish, Tibetan, Yoruba). Especially we tend to identify a culture with its language (French, German, Xhosa, Arabic, Greek, Quechua).

But you have likely already realized that each of those larger entities above is really a composite of smaller entities. America has the South, New England, California, the Midwest. Christianity is Catholic and A.M.E. Zion and Pentecostal and Episcopalian. We have socioeconomic classes. Then each occupation has its own culture: stockbrokers and police officers and academics and musicians and athletes and fast-food workers and farmers. Languages especially are collections of varieties: English is Cockney and Broadcast Standard (either BBC or NBC) and Black English Vernacular (BEV) and computer terminology and Valley Girl and formal academic and Chicano and a Harvard accent and sports cliches.

Probably the most common way to conceptualize these varieties is as subcultures underneath the greater culture (and linguistically as dialects and subdialects under the standard language), that is, to arrange them vertically into hierarchies. People with more money or power or prestige are upper-class, superior to lower-class people at the base; BEV or Brooklynese or underworld slang are lower than proper English. But these vertical arrangings are only *metaphors*, a way of speaking or thinking. Although sometimes a corporation will symbolize this by having its executives' offices on the highest floor, a person labeled as superior is very rarely physically higher. Metaphors of verticality are fictions, perhaps convenient fictions, but not quite really actual truths.

These metaphors pervade the language. We use them to denote magnitudes that aren't really vertical. When buying a gallon of gasoline costs more dollars than before we say *the price has gone up*; when buying shares of stock costs more dollars than before we say *the market is rising*. Musical sounds with more vibrations per second are *higher* than those with fewer. We turn the volume *up* to make the sound louder, the thermostat *up* to make the room warmer and *down* to make it cooler, but the air conditioner *up* to make it colder. When children perform better in school, we say they have *higher* grades (unless the curriculum has been *dumbed down*).

Nor are magnitudes the only categories identified by metaphors of verticality. North is *up*; south is *down*. Going against a flow is *upriver* or *upwind*. An easy task is *downhill*. A victor triumphs *over* the loser. After *high* school, you might proceed to *higher* education. Professional success is *up the ladder*; failure is a *downfall*. If you are more prosperous than your parents, you are enjoying *upward* mobility. Humans are *higher* animals than slugs or birds or insects, even though birds or insects are often physically higher than humans. Tragedy or epic is *high*; comedy or punk rock is *low*. Joyfulness is *high spirits*; unhappiness is *down* or *depression*. Euthanizing racehorses is *putting them down*; deprecating people is *putting them down*. Someone you have contempt for is *beneath* you; someone you admire you *look up to*. Love is a *higher* passion than *base* sex.

You have probably noticed that most of these metaphors of verticality have implied value judgments attached to them: up is good, down is bad; Heaven is up, hell is down. (There are exceptions: *deep* is better than *superficial*; *down to earth*, whatever that means, is usually a compliment). But these *sub*conscious value judgments, which are often covert (that is, *under the surface*), are dangerous. To refer to somebody else's group as a *sub*culture is often subtly to *downgrade* it, however unintentionally, or at least to suggest it is a lesser part of a greater and presumably better whole.

Metaphors of verticality are not the only metaphors of space we use to express relationships and judgments among entities. Another is the center-and-periphery metaphor, wherein something at the center of something is conceived of as being more real, more important, more salient, more *central*, that is, better, than something at the periphery or *margins*. The *core*, the *nucleus*, something *at the heart, in the mainstream* seems more real or authentic or enduring somehow than something *at the edge, near the border, off to the side*. Our concept of normal and abnormal originates from a center-and-periphery metaphor, for statistical data center themselves around a *norm* and everything away from that is labeled *abnormal*. Then "normal" moves from being a statistical term to one implying health, morality, and all kinds of rightness. (*Right* and *dexterous, left-handed* and *sinister* are also cognitively orienting metaphors of space with value judgments underhandedly attached.) If we feel that the *central* equals *superior* and the *peripheral* equals *inferior*, then center-and-periphery metaphors are vertical metaphors rendered in two dimensions and horizontally.

Center-and-periphery metaphors are the driving mechanism, and/or outward articulation, of egocentrism and ethnocentrism. Sociolinguistically, center-and-periphery metaphors occur as the belief that one's own variety of speech is the true or central language and all things else are variants or dialects, *marginal* and *inferior*, especially if one's speech approaches some mythical creature called the Standard.

The final spatial metaphor I am considering here is *inside* and *outside*. Someone you like or accept is *inside* your group, which may even be an *in-group*; everybody else would be *outsiders, beyond the pale, outlanders*, even *outlaws, outcasts*, or *out-castes*. Sometimes this is a simple binary, either/or: self or others, *inclusion* or *exclusion*. *Inside-and-outside* is the center-and-periphery metaphor with a distinct boundary.

The strongest version of this is the grammatical distinction between first and third person: *We* and *them*. The Constitution of the United States begins "We the people"; the giant ants in a 1954 science fiction movie are called *Them!*. Creatures labeled "Them" are often not simply others but are conceived negatively; we define "Them" by what we are *not* (and perhaps what we fear we might be). Thus *Them's* giant ants are also clearly a metaphor for any threat to humanity—or what we imagine or wish humanity to be.

Depending on context and nuance, the grammatical second person *you* might mediate the separation between third and first person. This is especially so in those languages that observe a distinction between polite and intimate second persons, like German's *Sie* and *du*, French's *vous* and *tu*, Spanish's *Usted* and *tu*, earlier English's *ye* and *thou*. That is why Martin Buber writes of *I-thou* relationships and why in this essay I so often address you as *you*.

Other metaphors are possible. One is the *organic* metaphor, wherein a culture is rendered as an organism—the *body politic*—and the components of the body politic are conceived as organs (head, limbs, lifeblood, nerve center, heart, muscles, digestive system) within an organically functioning whole. Menenius uses this metaphor at the beginning of Shakespeare's *Coriolanus* (Shakespeare got this metaphor from Plutarch, and it was traditional enough to be a cliche when it got to Plutarch). One then applies to the culture the terminology appropriate to a living organism: it is *healthy* or *moribund, reinvigorated* or *sterile, reborn, young* or *mature, growing*, maybe even *marrying* with other cultures, perhaps *fertilized* by external influences or *nourished* by *fruitful* institutions. Note that the term *organization* itself, which seems to be a neutral, abstract term, is really part of this metaphor system and thus carries along with it some covert value judgments. One trouble with this metaphor is that it can be used exploitively to suppress dissent—as Menenius does—by subordinating the elements of the society one designates as the muscles or stomach to the elements one designates as the head or the heart. (There is also this traditional joke. When the body was first created, each organ contended for who would be in charge. The head said it should be in charge because it did all the thinking. The heart thought it should be because it controlled the blood and was the designated seat of noble feelings. The stomach said it should be because it processed the food that enabled the whole body to function. The anus, however, said nothing at all but just closed up. After a few days everything backed up and all the organs got so bollixed that they just conceded. That's why, today, in all organizations the assholes are in charge.)

Another possible metaphor system is to conceive of culture as a *textile*, wherein the components or tendencies are *threads woven* together. If one were to refer to the well-integrated diversity of a culture it would be a *tapestry*; if one were to refer to a less well-integrated culture, it would be a *crazy quilt* (*mosaic* is a similar but not altogether equivalent metaphor). One is *clothed* in or by one's culture and *knit up* with its institutions and other people. So if one is worried about the *fabric* of a culture, one might speak of it being *torn* or *rent asunder*: indeed, this book was prompted by concern that our society might possibly be *unraveling*.

If metaphors are so pervasive and potentially so pernicious because they express value judgments, usually *down-putting* value judgments, that are unacknowledged and thus not up for review, can anything be done about them? For one thing, we can recognize them as metaphors, fictions, and not as reality. (If you have borne with me thus far, then we have to some extent already done that, and consciousness has been *raised*.) Since metaphors, by their very nature, describe something in terms that it is not, can we eliminate them altogether? Maybe mystics or the Buddha can think without metaphors, although they cannot render those thoughts to the rest of us without some sort of metaphor, but for most of us the language and our cognitive processing are so addicted to metaphors that we probably cannot do without them. The best I can do is to offer a methadonic substitute metaphor that I call

The Allegory of the Gameroom

Imagine that you are in a giant room with all kinds of games to play: basketball, bridge, Mortal Kombat, dice, chess, football, figure skating, soccer, poker, Scrabble, baseball, the dozens, archery, Go Fish, drag racing, Wall Street, tic-tac-toe, softball, Trivial Pursuit, long jumping, Jeopardy—anything you can think of and some you can't. (Throughout I am defining the term *game* loosely and broadly: I will make my meaning clear as I go along, but if my conception and yours are not quite congruent, that is all right.) Any equipment you need—cards, balls, pads, computer—will be there. You can switch around from one game to another with varying degrees of conscious choice. The games will vary from being pure chance (dice) to pure skill (chess), but most games (poker, baseball, golf) will have some admixture of chance and skill. Some games you will be better at than others. Some games you will prefer, probably those games you are better at or more accustomed to. You will play the games with varying degrees of intensity: winning will sometimes matter very much and sometimes not very much at all. Sometimes you will play for prizes; sometimes you will play for the sake of playing well; sometimes you will play just for the satisfaction of playing the game for its own sake; and sometimes you will play only for the sake of playing with other people.

But you must always be playing some game, in the rules of this allegory, except maybe when you are asleep. Even time-outs are part of the structure of the game. Sometimes you will have teammates. And you must always be playing with other people, perhaps with many people as in football or marathon running, or with only one as in checkers or boxing. Sometimes that other person may not be physically present; sometimes that other person may be an imaginary construct, as when you test your skill against the designer of an electronic game or the composer of a crossword puzzle. Sometimes that other person could be a simulacrum or another version of yourself, as when a runner tries to better her previous best time or a golfer tries to have a lower score than he did the last time he played this course.

Your competitors are also your colleagues. A boxer will do his utmost to defeat, maybe even injure, his opponent but without that opponent there is no bout—he can't play the game. The New York Knicks and the Chicago Bulls may hate each other on the court and even off, but they need each other because without them there would be no basketball game at all.

And without denying the normal human greed, corruption, residual bigotry, and even violence, it may be no accident that playing games, from the Olympic games (ancient and modern) to the contemporary Internet cybergames, is one of the very few areas of human life where apparently different kinds of people can and do operate together. Larry Bird, Michael Jordan, and Charles Barkley may be intense competitors while in a basketball game but friendly collaborators in the game of selling hamburgers in a television commercial. No two people would appear to be more different than the African American trash-talking Charles Barkley and the Japanese Tokyo-trashing Godzilla (some few people might even deny that Godzilla is human), but after their fierce basketball game they walk off together with Barkley's arm around his competitor and colleague. Surely that is an improvement over Bensonhurst or the Balkans. For that matter, the worldwide popularity of both American basketball and Japanese Godzilla movies should help us realize the interpermeability of cultural values and artifacts.

The imprecision of the prepositions of conventional English underscores this collegiality of competitors: you can be said to be playing *against* your opponents but you are at least as likely to be said to be playing *with* them. Kasparov plays against Karpov and with him. The pseudosport pro wrestling reveals this most clearly: if you can clear your mind of the illusion that those wrestlers are genuinely competing, you will see them cooperatively taking turns beating up on each other, alternating between actively dishing out and actively taking.

What makes this paradox of cooperating competitors possible, what brings together even the most intense antagonists, are the rules of each game. In basketball, for example, the rules declare how many points go with which shot, what constitutes a successful shot, how many people are on a team, how the ball is to be handled, what is in bounds and what is out, what is a foul, how long the game lasts, who wins, and what the official penalties are for violating the rules. Both sides follow the rules; by prescribing activity the rules not just facilitate the game but enable it. Indeed, the structuralists would argue that the rules *are* the game. I agree, but I would add that the games and their rules don't exist unless and until people are playing them.

Furthermore, each game has, broadly speaking, two kinds of rules, which I am here calling the Rules and the RULES. The Rules are what you will find in the official rulebook; they are formal, more or less consciously known by everybody, enforced by referees. But part of the game is to get away with evading some of the Rules. In football, for example, holding your opponent is against the Rules, but holding occurs on nearly every play—the game within the game is how much you can get away with holding. In bridge, the Rules forbid communicating information to your partner with facial expressions or pauses between bids, but because it's probably impossible to avoid completely, and nearly everybody does it anyway, the question is how egregiously it's done. The RULES delineate what is beyond the game, beyond what the rulebook says, what people know and observe unconsciously, and what puts them outside the game when they violate the RULES. Sometimes the RULES permit more than the Rules do and sometimes less, but the RULES are more inexorable than the Rules. In basketball you can hit your opponent with an elbow up to the point when you do it too much and a foul is called, within the Rules, but if you stab him with a knife that is against the RULES. In figure skating, the Rules specify what kind of music you can have, how long your program lasts, which jumps are required, which are permitted, and which are forbidden, what kind of contact is permitted between partners in pairs skating, but the RULES won't let you hit your opponent's knee with a riot baton. The crucial difference between the Rules and the RULES is that you can break the Rules (perhaps with a specified penalty being assessed) and still be playing the game but you can't break the RULES and still be playing the game.

When you are playing a game, the Rules may seem natural or primordial or God-given, but actually they are customary or arbitrary, specific to each game. There is no inherent reason why a basketball rim must be ten feet above the floor or a chess bishop must go on a diagonal or the scoring in tennis goes love-15-30-40-game or spades outrank hearts in bridge (as they do not in poker or gin rummy), except that those games would not be basketball or chess or tennis or bridge otherwise. But the arbitrariness of the Rules of each game is very important, because that is why switching from game to game is possible: all you have to do is learn the Rules and RULES of each new game. Natural laws like the second law of thermodynamics or biological instinct cannot be undone: if you are a sparrow you cannot play at being a banana slug. But if you are a basketball player, you can learn the Rules of roulette or golf or baseball and play them too, even if not as well.

The most important thing of all is that, just as you and your teammates are linked by playing together, you and your opponents are linked, so you and the people playing even the other games are also linked. For, in the allegory at least, we are all playing some sort of game: I call that *gameness*.

Each game has its own language. A *hit* is different in baseball and boxing; *hitting the wall* is literal in automobile racing and handball but metaphoric in marathon running. A *hook* is good in boxing and basketball but bad in golf, and metaphoric in all. Greg Louganis should *take a dive*, but a boxer who does breaks the RULES. Linguistics and billiards mean different things by the term *English*.

Each language has its own Rules and RULES. The Rules are conventions of appropriate diction. The RULES are the very structure of a language—the syntax, phonology, morphology, and lexicon (what together linguists call the *grammar*). *Ain't no better way to say it* violates the Rules of some games—and obeys the Rules of others—but never violates the RULES of language because any speaker of English will understand it, even those who don't approve of it. *Ain't no better way to say it* is still playing the game of speaking English. But **ulgk the the natln are niznt dunkdink ua of* violates the RULES of English and most probably any other language. It doesn't communicate; it isn't playing the game.

Although no two people use the exact same language, when you and someone else speak languages similar enough to be mutually intelligible, you are playing a language game and/or using language to play your other games. The lingo of each game might be more suitable for it than for other games, but that does not make it superior. Furthermore, you can learn and use the language appropriate for each game as you switch around. In the movie *Bull Durham* one of the tasks of the veteran baseball player is to teach the new rookie the cliches.

And just as people playing different games are linked by gameness, so people using different languages are linked by *languageness*, the distinctively human ability and proclivity to use language at all. (Linguists call this *languageness* "linguistic competence"; and that all undamaged people have linguistic competence has been an article of faith and working assumption for linguistics at least since Noam Chomsky's 1957 linguistic revolution. Some linguists posit and search for a universal grammar that underlies all languages and therefore all peoples.)

One more thing about games before we connect this allegory to the Rules of this book: games incorporate and encourage individual stylishness beyond their Rules. A lay-up or routine jump shot is worth two points by the basketball Rules but a 360 in-your-face two-handed backwards jammin' slam dunk goes beyond the Rules' two points. Willie Mays and Joe DiMaggio are appreciated for the grace of their fielding as well as for getting the batter out. Figure skating and diving are won or lost nearly entirely on artistic style. Some chess combinations are more elegant than others; in bridge a strip and throw-in is more beautiful than cashing out tricks. The RULES give more credit for style than the Rules do. Unlike the six points for a touchdown in football or the twenty points for a minor suit overtrick in bridge, which are specified by the Rules, how much credit you get for style depends on the tastes of the spectators. On what basis the spectators form their tastes, and thereby their judgments, is beyond my knowledge and therefore beyond the scope of this essay, but that basis is probably mostly social: people tend to like what their cultures have taught them to like.

Now, while each game in the gameroom has its own set of equipment, number of participants, degree of chance or skill, competition, cooperation with others, Rules, RULES, language, and style, the important thing that *underlies* them all is their *overarching* gameness (metaphors of verticality do not have to be logically consistent). You are all, always, playing one game or another—in the allegory, that is. But my proposition here is that each culture with its own set of equipment, number of participants, degree of chance or skill, competition, cooperation with others, Rules, RULES, language, and style is very much like a game. (And vice versa: each game is its own culture.) As with some games, the people who are part of your culture are not always physically present. For the overarching, underlying condition is the same for all of us: we are all, always, playing in one form of culture or another.

This allegory of the gameroom is only an extended metaphor for culture, and like all metaphors it is partly misleading. For one thing, culture may be more serious and less fun than games, with more consequential outcomes. Political activity, especially in those cultures that have electoral politics, looks very much like a spectator sport. But seeing politics as a spectator sport risks downplaying the importance and real consequences of politics: politics can be a matter of literal life or death, and even in those cultures where the losers are not shot or beheaded, politics is a major determinant of resource allocation, so that politics can affect the quality of life even where it does not completely effect the existence of it.

And it may be easier to learn the Rules of a different game than the RULES of another culture. RULES are probably mostly subconscious, so they are harder to learn than conscious directions, although RULES can be made accessible to the conscious through scholarship, criticism, and education. It is like language: linguists have established a Critical Age Hypothesis, which posits that children can best learn languages between the ages of about two to twelve, and it is probably no coincidence that children can learn new games and move from culture to culture more easily than adults can. Some things we can learn from children better than they learn from us.

Nor is this allegory value-free, any more than any other system of metaphor is value-free. It's a rhetoric designed to impose or smuggle in my values. By casting cultures and languages as games I might be reducing the premium put upon culture. I am doing this for the sake of diversity of outlook, flexibility of behavior, and tolerance for others, but those are still values, and they are values somewhat antithetical to the values of loyalty to one's group or subordination to one's heritage.

But at least the allegory of the gameroom is not sub-rosa like spatial metaphors. And while one may have one's favorite games (probably the ones one is most familiar with), there is nothing inherent or natural about any particular game to make it even appear to be superior to any other game. And that is my main point: the allegory of the gameroom does not prefer any one culture to another. As my late colleague Izola Young said, "Different does not mean inferior."

Moreover, another reason not to assert the superiority of some cultures over others is that, just as in the allegory you can play many games, each of us is every day in several cultures. Most of us are playing in the culture of some nation-state (though many people—Palestinians, Bosnians, refugees from all over—do not have a nation-state to call their own). Each of us is playing in the culture of some ethnic group; and most of us are in a religion and a sect of that religion. Each occupation forms its own culture: if you are a lawyer and I am an academic, we are each playing by the Rules and RULES of our particular professions (note that occupational cultures most clearly resemble games and are sometimes overtly nicknamed "games": "the insurance game," "the pajama game," not to mention "the mating game"). Then each individual company or law firm or academic department will have its own specific culture game.

Your household is its own culture, though participating in the other cultures, and that household might sometimes divide into the adults' culture and the children's. There are temporary cultures; the neighborhood bar, perhaps, or a social club or the crowd at a sporting event or the salesroom of a car dealership or a classroom or even a chance conversation.

The point of all of this is that, just as in the allegory of the gameroom, you can, and every day you do, move from one culture to another, as you switch from the styles and languages of the workplace to the home to the church to the street. We are all, each of us, always and already multicultural.

And each culture is transmitted, packaged, identified by its own language. Unhappily, not only is each culture marked by its own language but many cultures, and the individuals within them, are stigmatized—put down (and held down economically)—by the language they use. Or rather it is much more accurate to say that they are put or held down not by the languages themselves but by the attitudes of other people toward those languages. Eliza Doolittle knows this. African Americans know this. Hispanic Americans know this. Asian Americans know this. Previous generations of immigrants knew this. Southerners and Appalachians know this. Deborah Tannen is only the most prominent among many linguists who have demonstrated that women know this. Students who don't write textbook English know this.

But any up-to-date linguistics textbook will tell you that no human languages, including the ones alleged to be substandard, are inferior to any other. Conversely, no human languages, including the ones alleged to be Standard, are superior. All languages are equally expressive, communicative, grammatical, flexible, adaptive, user-friendly, and abstraction-capable. Because language use is just like game playing: each language or dialect may be different but each has both Rules and RULES. We humans are united by the overarching, underlying use of language.

Part of playing language games is using style. Of course, some people can use language more stylishly than others (Edmund Spenser, Jesse Jackson, Jane Austen, Nikki Giovanni, Vladimir Nabokov for a few examples among many). But it is important to realize that your judgment on a game player's style is a matter of taste, and dislike of one style of language may be a misperception of which game is being played (the language of each occupation is *technical terminology* if you respect it, *jargon* if you don't). For style in language is part of the RULES of the game and effective style might not always subordinate itself to the Rules.

One of these temporary cultures is you reading this essay in this book and me writing it. And we are participating in the other cultures that make this temporary culture possible. Although I have not specified my sources, much of this essay has been handed down and adapted from others, present and not. We share the same language, English, for example, including some of the conventions, or Rules, of writing (except that we have slightly different idiolects: for example, unless you care about linguistics, you are much less likely than I am to use the term *idiolect*, which means each person's individual way of using language). Furthermore the intellectual values, educational system, technological resources, and commercial potential of the culture made it possible for my co-contributors and the editor to produce this book and you to obtain it. And because you and I share the same culture and are (now) playing the same game, we can both know who Eliza Doolittle is and what hitting a figure skater in the knee with a riot baton signifies.

Moreover, in the culture of reading this book, you and I are playing a game right now. Each of my assertions is a rhetorical move to make a point (intellectually) and to score points (in the game). Some will score and some won't, according to the Rules of intellectual discourse and your judging. We are certainly collaborating: you need me to write this and I need you to read it. We are also competing when you try to think of better points than the ones I make. If, like a cornerback or boxer, you try to anticipate my rhetorical moves, then I, like a wide receiver or boxer, try to anticipate your anticipating. And you can quit at any time and move on to some other game.

As one of my rhetorical moves in this game I have chosen a particular style of language, a postmodern, paronomasial, somewhat self-conscious style with lots of first- and second-person pronouns, somewhere between the academic and the informal registers, that is either within the Rules of the game or seeks to get away with bending them (like trying to get away with using the word *asshole*). So "Metaphor, Language, Games, Cultures" is itself a metaphor, game, allegory, and culture within and representing the allegory of the gameroom.

Although my concern is mostly linguistic and epistemological, the rules and referees of this book require that I set out the political implications of the metaphors, or metaphor-systems, that I have presented for contemplating cultures.

Any metaphor is a fiction, an interpretation or even a distortion of reality (whatever reality may be), and any one metaphor or even system of metaphors will be, at best, only a partial depiction. The first political implication then is to be aware that our metaphor-systems may be signs of the way we organize perceptions and subconsciously assign values (of course, in this case "we" means everybody else, not you and me). To the extent that we act on and establish our polity on one of these metaphor-systems we are founding on a fiction, an illusion, a delusion. This isn't all that bad, especially since it is probably unavoidable, as long as we are all aware of what we are doing and do not confuse a linguistic and rhetorical habit with actual reality. One doesn't have to know what actual reality is (I don't) to be alert to the metaphoric nature of our ways of articulating it. And certainly we ought not use those metaphors as devices, unconscious or not, to alienate one person or group from another.

The second political implication comes from the temporariness of cultures, by which I mean both that each person moves from culture to culture and that each culture changes. When you cease reading this essay or this book you will move on to some other culture. As each of us moves in and out of cultures, we must remember that others are too; no culture can be—or even is—completely either inclusive or exclusive. But even the grander cultures, less ephemeral than this essay or this book, change: the Western civilization of Hesiod and Virgil differs from that of Virginia Woolf and Steven Spielberg; Lao Tsu's China is not the same as Mao's or Deng's. (Whether these changing cultures retain some kind of permanent core culture is too big a question for me except to observe the center-and-periphery metaphor again). So we ought not fix, design, imagine a polity depending on an assumption of eternity, either in origin or in destiny. Earlier in this essay I said "culture may be more serious. . .than games" rather than "is more serious" because in some thought systems, notably religious ones, culture is little more than a game when viewed from the perspective of eternity—postmodern decadence and medieval Boethian Christianity may have some common ground after all.

The third political implication is that, while there are different games, languages, cultures, and styles, before all that we have a common gameness, languageness, cultureness, and styleness, not in their existential diversities but in the essential humanness that we all play games, use language, are in cultures, appreciate style. The analogy is with food: each culture has its distinctive cuisine and the games it plays with food, yet anybody can eat and enjoy some other culture's food, because before the diversity is the common human need both for nutrition and the sensual pleasure of flavor. All humans are inherently cultural, and multicultural. But the important thing is cultureness, not any particular culture, just like languageness, gameness, and styleness are each more important than specifically English, basketball, or Neo-Classicism.

Raising our awareness of all the metaphors we use and the games we play should lower our feeling of threatening differentness.

Chapter 3

Shattered Images: From Consensus to Contention in Classic American Film

Sam B. Girgus

The images of the film's opening scenes immediately convey director George Stevens's intentions. The wide screen and deep focus present more than a dramatic picture; they also comprise a statement. Indeed, the very letters of the title lengthen before our eyes, stretching into the distant horizon, inscribing an ideology on the landscape in a manner that marries visual and verbal signs—*Giant.* Stevens presents us with a visual metaphor for America and for the dynamics of the American idea itself. Expansion. Growth. Diversity. Consensus. The director constructs a Texas of the mind that epitomizes the progress of the American system. Based on the best-selling Edna Ferber novel of 1950, the very title, *Giant,* signifies America as an ever-expanding home, an endless geography to house, protect, and to provide sanctuary and asylum for all of the world's people; America as an infinite idea of assimilation and rebirth; but also America as colossus, grotesque in imperialistic desires and an unappeasable appetite for domination and control.

Given the year of its release, 1956, the opening scene of *Giant* renders a kind of visual climax for the way a generation of directors envisioned America. It constitutes a moment of visual blatancy that perfectly summarizes a pervasive ideological perception for such directors as Frank Capra and John Ford as well as Stevens. Here Stevens develops visual space to dramatize an ideology of consensus and inclusion that emerged triumphant for America with the victory over Nazism during the Second World War, only to be challenged once again by the freeze of the Cold War during its most stinging days in the mid-1950s. In the work of these and other mainstream directors, American history becomes an unbroken continuum marking steady progress from the days of discovery to the revolution, through the Civil War, up to the present moment of history.

Moreover, along with this linear and lateral development of American history through an expanding horizon of conquest and opportunity, there also occurs another movement of vertical inclusion of ever-growing numbers of people to be included in the American Way. The imagery of Crèvecoeur's "new American" as symbolic of a new race consisting of all peoples, of Paine's belief in America as a Noah's Ark literally beginning history all over again, of the utopian notion of the American garden as an asylum for all the world's peoples manifests itself in the minds and works of these directors. Again, the screen image of *Giant* brilliantly dramatizes this congeries of ideas and beliefs pertaining to the symbolism of the American landscape and America as an "ism," an ideology for a particular nation and the world.

Indeed, this ideology of consensus and inclusion informs and energizes the lengthy narrative of *Giant* as it rather heavy-handedly dramatizes the political message of overcoming racist and reactionary attitudes by liberalizing the position and role of minorities, women, and even children in American society. It clearly advocates the inclusion of minorities within the American dream and condemns corporate greed and exploitation as dramatized by the character played by James Dean. The film stands ahead of its time in its representation of the modern liberal woman, as portrayed by Elizabeth Taylor, who guides her husband, played by Rock Hudson, away from the values and proclivities of a decadent and violent macho mentality no longer deemed appropriate for the modern industrial and atomic age.

At the same time, the film's visualization of an ideology of consensus and expansion also suggests a subtext of crisis. Implicit in the visualizations of the ideology of *Giant* is the theme of the need to repel the alleged domination and expansionism of Americanism. A Cold War-era message at the core of the film implies the need to modify aggressive nationalism and domination. Stevens, a liberal who fought against loyalty oaths in Hollywood and faced McCarthy-era criticism, apparently perceives a dangerous and negative side to the mindset of the Texas *Giant* metaphor for America. *Giant* undermines the very expansionism and power that it visually celebrates and questions the conformity and control that occur through the ideology of consensus that it extols.

The film, therefore, dramatizes a consensus ideology at war with itself. *Giant* tries to achieve ethnic and gender diversity through consensus, while also seeking ideological and cultural vigor through restraint, compromise, and accommodation. The film articulates a complex ideological dialogue and situation that reinforces the tension at the core of liberal ideology during an age of international and multicultural responsibility. It wants to promulgate causes of economic responsibility, social equality, and welfare without sacrificing too much of the mystique behind the old-fashioned values of American dynamism and growth that are manifest in the film's opening moments and throughout its glamorized presentation of Texas and its people.

As played and developed by Dennis Hopper, the character of Hudson's and Taylor's son brilliantly demonstrates the film's ideological ambivalence and uncertainty. Hopper epitomizes and articulates the film's liberal ideological position. He instinctively feels responsibility and compassion for others and minorities. He rebels against his father's demands for him to fulfill classic conceptions of Texas cowboy masculinity by rejecting a life on the ranch in favor of a career in medicine that will give him the opportunity to serve and care for the disadvantaged. As a liberal personality, Hopper appears as tender, caring, and sensitive. Most important, he marries, outside of his class and culture, an Hispanic woman and immediately begins a family with her. In terms of narrative and character development, Hopper obviously occupies the film's most liberal ideological position. Indeed, Hudson ultimately demonstrates acceptance of his new daughter-in-law and the marriage through his use of Hispanic epithets as terms of endearment for his grandchildren and his ferocious fight with a restaurant owner who won't serve an Hispanic family. However, any pretense of heroism, independence, initiative, and moral strength that Hopper gains within the story is immediately dissipated by the visual presentation of Hopper's body and his acting. The contrast powerfully demonstrates the true complexity of Hollywood cinema. The divergence between the narrative and the mise-en-scène in the form of Hopper's figure and acting reveals the multiple level of meanings to be considered in film. Thus, while Hopper voices the liberal ideology of the film, he subverts the potential power of this position by appearing physically weak, wimpish, and whiny and personally soft and irrelevant, especially when juxtaposed against the looming figure of Hudson as a man who can change without losing classic Hollywood marks of masculine strength and solidity.

Moreover, this representational complexity and ideological conflict in *Giant* also can be discerned in the works of other directors. The pervasive presence of this conceptual tension within classic Hollywood cinema indicates an ideological complexity to these films that parallels their artistic ingenuity and the complexity of the times. As Hudson and Taylor physically and dramatically age before our eyes, they appear to be reconciled to the idea that such tensions will persist and remain unresolved in both their own lives and in the nation. However, while they seem reasonably content as aging relics, the film's inability to articulate an ideological alternative to such persisting tension foreshadows the paralysis of consensus since the Vietnam era of discontent and the concomitant emergence of a cinema of fragmentation and disunity.

Accordingly, the opening shot and scene of *Giant* do not use visual technique to create or impose the ideology of Americanism upon an innocent spectator or audience in a manner reminiscent of traditional propaganda. They merely climax the various expressions of the same ideology of consensus and expansionism in innumerable other films. This shot and the film as a whole fulfill the thrust of decades of representation of American values and beliefs on the screen. Years of Hollywood filmmaking anticipate the graphic visualization of the hegemony of the American idea in *Giant* during this historic period of post-World War II triumph over fascism and confrontation with communism. In addition, in classic Hollywood film, cinematic creativity as evidenced in *Giant* consistently sustains the complex representation of ideology.

Thus, in *Mr. Smith Goes to Washington,* Capra constructs a different way to render Stevens's ideological code. A variation of the famous Kuleshov effect in the form of dramatic editing and montage as well as the construction of mise-en-scène achieves the same effect of an expansive ideology of consensus in Capra's film. Technology, art, and ideology cohere. Although the visual style, directing technique, and use of the camera differ radically from Stevens's opening long take, the ideology of cultural consensus, historical continuity, and national unity persists. Moreover, Capra's film also conveys the elements of complexity, dialogue, and contradiction that manifest themselves in Stevens's film. Instead of the vast, open spaces of Texas, Capra manipulates time and space to contain and intensify the world of America's bigness and inclusion within his tightly designed rendition of the Lincoln Memorial. In this comparison of directors, we visually go from Texas as a national state of mind to entering the mind of Lincoln, presented here visually and architecturally as a synecdoche of the American soul.

Significantly, a famous, melodramatic tour of the historic sites of Washington introduces the scene at the Lincoln Memorial. In this sequence, Capra provides a memorable compression of American history, giving us a stream of images of national founders and heroes and the writing of inspiring documents, all to the accompaniment of an evocative sound track of patriotic music designed to direct the audiences' emotion. The manipulation of time and space dramatizes the meaning of America as blatantly as Stevens's long take that opens *Giant.* Capra's montage and elliptical editing lengthen the story time of the film to include the nation's founding, in effect extending the film's narrative to include much of American history. This visual rendering of American history, in combination with the stirring music, forms an ideological stream of sights and sounds that carries Jimmy Stewart up the stairs and into the temple of democracy, the Lincoln Memorial.

Capra, then, initially dwarfs Stewart within the Memorial, making him part of a greater moment in history, and positioning him between enormous pillars that emphasize the religious and monumental significance of this cultural environment. The lighting, of course, further contributes to the religious and awesome quality of the scene. However, instead of constriction and confinement, the cramped physical space between the massive pillars and the balanced geometry of light and shadow become comforting; we are resting in the cradle of democracy, supported spiritually by powerful, unseen but deeply felt forces that inform and enlighten, and ultimately, save us. Small and diminished in terms of his own physical size, Mr. Smith discovers himself to be part of an intellectual and ideological vastness greater than even Stevens's Texas contains. He becomes part of an historic and institutional system of national and religious inevitability. The entry onto the scene of important ethnic and cultural types clearly contributes to the development of the theme of consensus. The pageant of sight and sound of Smith's tour that precedes the visit to the Memorial becomes historically immediate and relevant with the appearance of a humble black man and an earnest man who looks Jewish. Smith looks at both with solemn approval, suggesting special appreciation for the elderly Jewish man who assists a young boy in reading the magnificent concluding words of the Gettysburg Address. In the latter days of the New Deal and in the midst of the Nazi tumult overseas, a Jew and a black man become part of Lincoln's America; they inherit, but also continue and perpetuate the line of history that brought them and Smith to the monument to worship the memory of Lincoln at the feet of the marvelous statue. Thus, tight spaces become the ideological equivalent of the vastness of the Texas plains.

Moreover, Capra also uses writing to inscribe ideology, just as Stevens in the later film uses the letters that form the word "Giant" to brand the landscape; but here the words on the screen are inscribed within the mind and consciousness of the participants rather than on the landscape. Lincoln's highlighted words on the monument are the words in Smith's mind, while the verbal utterances by the young boy as he reads aloud are interrupted by the elderly man's punctuating commentary of corrections, somewhat reminiscent of a Hebrew teacher. This scene amounts to a literal calling of the ideology to both Smith, the internal spectator, and the external spectator in the audience in a way that anticipates the radical speculations of Louis Althusser and his enthusiastic followers during the past two decades. The scene, however, suggests not just ideological calling or interpellating but dialogue, exchange between the words and memory of Lincoln and the characters at the Memorial as well as exchange between the viewing spectator and the events on the screen. While Lincoln's words confirm the director's didactic impulse behind Smith's tour and presence, the ironic and self-deprecating undertone throughout the movie suggests that Capra, the film's hidden guiding force, does not really deceive the audience into being involved and called into the film's ideology. The level of cinematic self-consciousness for this film, while representative of Hollywood's hidden-camera style, nevertheless also contains considerable self-awareness of its own devices, as when Stewart mistakes a lighted movie marquee for an historical monument.

The endless space of the opening scene of *Giant* and the control and manipulation of time and space in *Mr. Smith Goes to Washington* indicate the absence of real alternatives in both the films and the culture to the consensus of the American idea. The lack of apparent or attractive systems outside the universalism and individualism, independence and community of the American idea engenders strong commitment to that ideology. The films present this ideology as an all-encompassing envelope providing shelter and comfort. Both films also suggest the power of that ideology to convince, cohere, celebrate, and control. While inclusion compels certain forms of sacrifice and transformation, the films often dissemble the cost of that transformation beneath the enthusiasm for participation. Indeed, the films strongly suggest a compulsion to use the American idea as a means for control and uniformity.

Ford's *Drums along the Mohawk*, which appeared in 1939, the same year as *Mr. Smith Goes to Washington*, provides an extraordinary visual expression of political control and cultural domination. The elements of such hegemony that linger in the background of these other films surface prominently, although perhaps unintentionally, in Ford's film. In a moment of particular historic and cinematic irony, Ford dissimulates coercion and intimidation as apparent loyalty and unity. In the film, Henry Fonda and Claudette Colbert, among other frontier settlers during the Revolutionary War, celebrate a triumph over the British and hostile Indians, following a rescue scene that seems modeled directly after the notorious rescue in *Birth of a Nation* of white Southern womanhood by the Ku Klux Klan. Fonda and Colbert pause to examine, admire, and pay respect to the new flag that symbolizes their new country. In two powerful shots, Ford shows the reaction to this new flag of both a black woman slave and a friendly Indian chief. The Indian chief ceremoniously salutes the flag, while the black woman looks solemnly and with apparent awe and allegiance to it, her glance interlocking with the expressions of the free citizens. The slightest suggestion of uncertainty and ambiguity also can be found in her eyes and expression.

Through these gestures and looks, both slave and Indian appear to acquiesce to their placement and position within a history and culture that conquer and enslave them and their people. These shots in the film anticipate Roland Barthes's account in *Mythologies* of a black soldier saluting the French colors in a similar manner and for a similar purpose.[1] Perhaps radical and controversial in its own time as a sign of ethnic and racial participation, the gestures of support by the slave and Indian emblematize the hegemony of the American idea. What Ford apparently sees as voluntary gestures by the Indian chief and the black slave of support and loyalty to a higher authority, also exposes the internalization of social and ideological control. The benevolent and innocent face Ford puts on this process of inclusion only serves to dramatize the ideology's awesome power to incorporate and absorb difference. His apparent blindness to the demeaning portrayal in many of his films of the Irish, an ethnic group he favored and cherished as his own, suggests an element of denial regarding this sensitive issue of ethnic status within the dominant culture. His work in this area also dramatizes the self-referential, circular nature of the film's ideology as well as the depth of his commitment to it.

In effect, by trying to dramatize the ideology of consensus and cultural unity, Ford in these shots suggests the exact opposite—difference, dissensus, marginalization. He unwittingly foregrounds the very elements of opposition he wishes to obscure and repress at that precise moment. In doing so, he inadvertently advertises an issue also confronting Capra and Stevens as directors of democratic consensus. In looking backward to an overworked and exploited vision of America as a cultural and historical totality, the directors also deal with the contradictory and adversarial factors which challenge such unity.

The films of these directors, therefore, need to be studied again, not only to determine how they involve the spectator in the dominant value systems but also in terms of how they represent the marginal, the other. How do narrative and ideology function in them to position and represent difference and otherness? Do the films silence difference, as in the one instance already noted by Ford? Are minority vision and voice denied narrative authority in order to be incorporated within and to accede to a dominant view? Or can we find traces of genuine dialogue and debate in which positions of consensus and dissensus engage and contradict each other for the purpose of achieving original expression? These questions concerning ideology, ethnicity, and the representation of minority visions and voices are important, especially for these particular films and directors that are so strongly identified with the expression of American cultural and political dominance at mid-century.

Also, the works of these directors obviously are structured to place the viewer within the framework of American ideology. In a sense, they all attempt the impossible—the visual portrayal of an unrepresentable visual ideal, a utopian, and therefore unrealizable, picture of the composite American character. They propose a visual version of the American ideology of consensus and regeneration, a moving portrait of what sociologists and historians have termed universalism or exceptionalism, the idea that throughout history only America among the world's nations identifies itself ideologically, socially, and culturally as a people and homeland for all peoples. Verbally and ideologically seeming to contain and control the impulse toward difference and otherness in order to achieve hegemony and consensus, these films visually push boundaries and barriers of color, race, gender, and ethnicity. A Whitmanesque desire to contain multitudes alters stable and certain definitions of the cultural and ideological center as well as the margins between insiders and outsiders, us and them. A compelling ideal of universal representation, renewal, and inclusion seems to motivate the moving images of these classic Hollywood narratives toward a pragmatic consensus based on liberal, democratic faith.[2]

Inevitably, this thrust toward sameness, uniformity, and one-dimensionality in film and culture occurs with a counter tendency toward difference and heterogeneity. As in the case of Ford's film, the hegemonic drive toward ideological and cultural domination often foregrounds opposition and otherness. Moreover, recent critical trends in both film and literary studies help us to understand and analyze this process of ideological debate and incorporation. Close semiotic, psychoanalytical, and ideological readings and analyses of films demonstrate the true complexity and multiplicity of cinematic representation. Such critical readings and interpretations help turn films into battlefields of critical and cultural debate and discourse. These films, therefore, often contain within their moving representational images and structures powerful elements of fragmentation, dissensus, and disruption. Such disruption suggests the revelation in the films of the need for change and anticipates the drastic cultural and social dislocation since the Kennedy years. Examples abound of such complexity and anticipation. The changing role, situation, and position of women comprise the core of Capra's *Mr. Smith's Goes to Washington* and Stevens's *Woman of the Year.* Ethic complexity as part of the broader American experience manifests itself in these and other movies, while concerns about the very nature of selfhood, identity, and manhood are central to *It's a Wonderful Life, A Place in the Sun, Shane,* and innumerable other films of this era. Classic films frequently are themselves not only visual, aural, dramatic, and intellectual embodiments of cultural complexity and diversity operating on all the so-called tracks of film but also agents of change. While such films clearly propel a holistic, consensual notion of one Americanism for all, they often also indicate the end of a way of looking at America. They help to mark a transition in American film from hegemonic homogeneity to an awareness, understanding, and emphasis upon heterogeneous difference and otherness. Rather than suppressing or challenging such change, this generation of Hollywood directors often pioneered, consciously or inadvertently, in the presentation and institution of change on the whole range of issues confronting America. Efforts to control and contain movements toward difference and otherness often led to their dramatic representation rather than their dispersal, dissimulation, or dissolution.

In general, as Leo Braudy suggests, if we compare classic Hollywood films and directors with contemporary works, we move from consensus, stability, and privileged positioning to a cinema characterized by displacement, decentering, disruption, discontinuity; we go from seeking harmony and concordance in the midst of diversity to searching out and emphasizing the marginal, different—the other. We also move from the classic organization of narrative, space, and visual and auditory signs based on privileged perspective to a more decentered and splintered cinematic vision based on contemporary cultural fragmentation, contention, and disruption. The widely discussed and documented penchant of classic Hollywood cinema to disguise the presence of directors, the camera, and the positioning of the viewing spectator changes to at least partial recognition of the process itself; we get a heightening of the marks of ideological and psychological articulation that force upon the viewer increased self-awareness and social self-consciousness.

At the same time, it needs to be emphasized that considerable overlap occurs between classic and contemporary cinema. Just as classic cinema should not be reduced to a simplistic notion of its ideological treatment of social and cultural issues, so also it should not be seen as artistically or cinematically impoverished, the victim of a conservative cinematic ideology designed to impede and undermine artistic innovation and ideological independence. As already noted, the work of the classic directors anticipates the cinematic vision and innovation of contemporary directors, just as their treatment of social issues helped to create today's prevalent atmosphere for change. The roots for the cinema of innovation, ethnic diversity, and gender equality of Woody Allen, Spike Lee, Martin Scorsese, John Singleton, Mira Nair, Julie Dash, Quentin Tarantino, Elaine May, Allen and Albert Hughes can be found in the social vision and cinematic imagination of many of our classic directors. Thus, it seems significant that the Hughes brothers modeled the structure and narrative technique of *Menace II Society,* the intense drama of inner-city violence among African American youth, after Scorsese's film about Italian "wise guys" and hoodlums, *Goodfellas,* thereby indicating a continuity not only of style and form but also of the representation of ethnicity, alienation, violence, and minority differences. Such continuity also may proffer a tentative delineation of the formation of a new cultural consensus based on both cultural history and the history of cinema. Given Scorsese's stature as a director and his growing reputation as a student and historian of film, his work provides an excellent foundation for developing such consensus.

In fact, it can be argued that the works of classic directors helped to revisualize, reconceptualize, and reformulate basic areas of American life and thought, including: women, gender, and sexuality; ethnicity and race; selfhood and society. In the films already discussed here and in innumerable other classic works, reconsideration of the situation of women, of gender relationships, and of consensus ideology to include people of color also led to new representations of the self and subjectivity in the context of social and historic forces. The appeal to victimization to arouse audience sympathy for the underdog or little man in classic cinema has become what many today consider to be an obsessive theme in contemporary films. Nevertheless, in spite of such connections between classic and contemporary directors, it should be emphasized that for most classic directors the current collapse of consensus in both culture and cinema generally would imply a life and world of chaos and dystopia. Their films render occasional glimpses of such dissensus and dystopia that suggest the need for consensus. For the earlier generation of classic directors, the end of consensus regarding basic American values, cohesiveness, and community becomes Jimmy Stewart's nightmare of nonexistence and nonidentity in Capra's *It's a Wonderful Life* or John Wayne's endless and meaningless wandering in Ford's *The Searchers* or Montgomery Clift's loss of love and belief in Stevens's *A Place in the Sun* or Deborah Kerr's and Donna Reed's journey toward rejection and pathos in Fred Zinnemann's *From Here to Eternity*. Thus, a reconsideration of classic cinema in the light of the importance of cultural consensus could help ameliorate the particularism, fragmentation, and separation that characterize so much of contemporary cinema. The construction of consensus would help fulfill the vision of regeneration of our classic directors, while also sustaining and structuring the drive for change of the current generation of filmmakers.

---

[1] Roland Barthes, *Mythologies*, trans. Annette Lavers (New York: Hill and Wang, 1957), 116.

[2] This capacity of American ideology to supersede and co-opt the challenge of otherness and difference arouses the ire of many vociferous, even vituperative critics. Thus, what Fredric Jameson writes in his recent study of film and ideology (*The Geopolitical Aesthetic: Cinema and Space in the World System* (Bloomington: Indiana University Press, 1992) about the power of "Western relativisms" in general to absorb and incorporate even nugatory and contradictory adversarial forces applies most appropriately to the authority of the American idea to achieve hegemony over discordant elements. Jameson says:

> But Western relativisms—however internally jarring and contradictory—have always seemed to take place within some essential class homogeneity: the most dramatic eruptions of otherness—as in race or gender—always ultimately seeming to fold back into conflicts on the inside of a sphere whose true other or exterior eluded representation altogether. And that virtually by definition, since in the very moment in which a thought or impulse from that unrepresentable Outside enters the field of thought or discourse, it will already have been represented, and, henceforth belong to "us," can no longer be truly other or noumenal (198).

Works Cited

Barthes, Roland. *Mythologies,* trans. Annette Lavers. New York: Hill and Wang, 1957.

Bercovitch, Sacvan. *The American Jeremiad.* Madison: University of Wisconsin Press, 1978.

———. "The Rites of Assent: Rhetoric, Ritual, and the Ideology of American Consensus." *The American Self: Myth, Ideology, and Popular Culture.* Edited by Sam B. Girgus. Albuquerque: University of New Mexico Press, 1981, 5-42.

Braudy, Leo. *The World in a Frame: What We See in Films.* Chicago: University of Chicago Press, 1984.

Byars, Jackie. *All That Hollywood Allows: Re-reading Gender in 1950s Melodrama.* Chapel Hill: University of North Carolina Press, 1991.

Fischer, Lucy. *Shot/Countershot: Film Tradition and Women's Cinema.* Princeton, NJ: Princeton University Press, 1989.

Girgus, Sam B. *The Films of Woody Allen.* Cambridge: Cambridge University Press, 1993.

———. *The New Covenant: Jewish Writers and the American Idea.* Chapel Hill: University of North Carolina Press, 1984.

———."The New Ethnic Novel and the American Idea." *College Literature* 20 (October 1993): 57-72.

Haskell, Molly. *From Reverence to Rape: The Treatment of Women in the Movies.* New York: Penguin, 1974.

Jameson, Fredric. *The Geopolitical Aesthetic: Cinema and Space in the World System.* Bloomington: Indiana University Press, 1992.

McLuhan, Marshall. *The Mechanical Bride: Folklore of Industrial Man.* Boston: Beacon Press, 1951.

Sklar, Robert, and Charles Musser, eds. *Resisting Images: Essays on Cinema and History.* Philadelphia: Temple University Press, 1990.

Uricchio, William, and Roberta E. Pearson. *Reframing Culture: The Case of the Vitagraph Quality Films.* Princeton: Princeton University Press, 1993.

Williams, Linda. *Figures of Desire: A Theory and Analysis of Surrealist Film.* Berkeley: University of California Press, 1981.

Chapter 4

Literacy, Culture, and the Colonial Legacy

Victor Villanueva, Jr.

I can't imagine many academics these days would want to be aligned with Antonio Gramsci's traditional intellectuals. In his *Prison Notebooks* he calls them "the dominant group's 'deputies' exercising the subaltern functions of social hegemony and political government" (12). That's not very flattering. Yet it happens: the unwitting passing on of the "truths" of the State, the unwitting passing on of the truths of those in power, passed on through the schools as well as other institutions. It happens that sometimes academics use their rhetorical skills not to counter hegemony but to maintain it. There is, for example, a current fondness for postcolonial literature, a celebration of the multiculturalism that has arisen, phoenix-like, from the ashes of colonialism. But despite the truly interesting work that falls under the head of "postcolonialism," the very label seems to me unfortunate. It is unfortunate because postcolonialism does not apply to America. A postcolonialism, a time after colonialism, has not arrived for America geopolitically, economically, or even in terms of something I'd risk calling a national attitude. So espousing a "post" to colonialism runs the risk of our overlooking the colonial legacy which continues to affect America's people of color, the colonialism that continues to affect how we go about our literacy practices, how we espouse multiculturalism while engaging in something else, how we fall short of attaining the multiculturalism we desire.

The Legacy

The United States remains every bit a colonial power. Although this isn't the place to explore dependency theory (Frank) or world-systems theory (Wallerstein), those discussions suggest that distinctions between colonialism-as-military-strategy and colonialism-as-economic-necessity are not very helpful, except ideologically, as ways of maintaining popular support for continued international control (Ross and Trachte). Whatever America's justifications, its history of imperial expansion still finds expression in its having over four hundred military bases throughout the world, in its fourteen classical colonies in the Pacific, in its old-fashioned colonial control over the U.S. Virgin Islands and Puerto Rico (Baver, Fraser). Whether a matter of military strategy or economic necessity, America remains a phenomenal imperial power. And I bypass neocolonialism, the economic dependence that nearly negates the need for a military presence in colonized areas, where, again, America remains a world power.

Puerto Rico might be something of a symbol of U.S. colonialism. Sherrie Baver, in *The Political Economy of Colonialism*, provides a detailed study of recent colonial policies over Puerto Rico. Two examples from among the many she provides tell of the imperial power the United States continues to enjoy over the island and the extent to which U. S. policy maintains such power. Although I leave the details to Baver, it is enough to note President Clinton's 1993 threat to remove the tax loophole enjoyed by industries who locate on the island, thereby sealing the island's fate to one of complete dependence, a dependence that has existed since the acquisition of the island through the Spanish-American War. This is not exactly self-determinacy. The U.S. Congress, in fact, decided not to allow Puerto Rico any self-determination, when it halted the island's attempt to enter into the plebiscite process, the process whereby colonies decide whether to seek independence, statehood, or continued commonwealth status. With U.S. military forces located in Puerto Rico, the island remains a classic colony; with its dependence on American industry and social welfare, it suffers the status of neocolonialism; and with so many who can claim kinship to Puerto Rico, even those who might have never been to the island, even those who have never spoken Spanish, its people on the mainland suffer the alienation of internal colonialism.

Internal Colonialism

Internal colonialism is hardly a new idea. The concept can be dated back to Lenin in his work, *The Development of Capitalism in Russia*. Gramsci alludes to an internal colonialism in reference to northern attitudes concerning the southern peasantry ("The Southern Question," 28). "Internal colonialism" is the term used by Latin American sociologists in describing Amerindian regions (Hechter, 8-9). In the United States, Harold Cruse referred to "domestic colonialism" in a 1962 essay which was later reprinted in a 1968 collection of his essays titled *Rebellion or Revolution*. Kenneth Clark, in 1965, drew parallels between colonialism and conditions in Harlem. Then Stokely Carmichael and Charles Hamilton elaborated on the parallels between African-American oppression and colonialism in *Black Power*. By 1968, Senator Eugene McCarthy was referring to African Americans as a colonized people (Blauner, 177). Yet all this was almost exclusively in reference to African Americans, espoused most vocally by Black nationalists. Hegemonic forces being what they are, social scientists objected that the term "internal colonialism" was being used metaphorically and thereby misleadingly. They demanded more empirical analyses, hard evidence that the racism affecting African Americans was, in fact, a matter of colonialism. By 1975, references to internal colonialism in America, with the exception of American Indians (no minor exception, granted), were all but gone.

But whatever the academic vogue, America's people of color nevertheless reflect an ongoing internal colonialism. This is obvious when it comes to American Indians, residing in "domestic dependent nations" (K. Jensen, 156). Less obvious for most is internal colonialism as cultural domination, a kind of psychological domination. Many, if not most, of my Navajo and other

American Indian students, for example, were made to attend Bureau of Indian Affairs schools. There, they were forbidden to live with their families and clans, forbidden to speak their native tongues. A similar kind of internal colonialism can be seen to be operating when it comes to America's Latino populations, descendants of earlier American colonization. English-only legislation and attempts to do away with bilingual education mark a forced assimilation similar to that imposed on American Indians, a forced assimilation which is part of the makeup of colonialism. And there remain the parallels between social attitudes toward African Americans and the African-American ghettoes as matters of internal colonialism. For all of America's people of color, current literacy practices, despite desires for multiculturalism, suffer from a colonial legacy.

On the one hand, there is the wish to promote multiculturalism or pluralism; on the other, even the most liberal teaching methods tend to be assimilationist, especially in terms of language instruction. Intentions are good, assuming that linguistic and cultural assimilation leads to full participation within the society. But assimilation is a cultural flattening, the opposite of multiculturalism. And even when assimilation is achieved, full participation still tends to be denied the internally colonized. Ellis Cose describes the frustrations and anger among African Americans who have achieved economic success and positions of prestige yet continue to experience racism. I tell of one Latino's frustrations with continued racial or ethnic distinctiveness, despite having achieved all the trappings of full assimilation. Internal colonialism remains.

Assimilation

Complete, structural assimilation is not easily achieved, if it can be achieved at all for people of color. Mario Barrera explains the components of full assimilation by way of a theoretical model, which I modify. What emerges is a model containing three major components of complete structural assimilation:

1. The historical mode of entry into the dominant society by those seeking assimilation;

2. The number and distribution or concentration of those attempting to take part in the overall society; and
3. The racial and cultural characteristics of those seeking equity with the majority.

First: the mode of entry. If the mode of entry of the new group is voluntary, the new group does not carry the baggage of having become part of the United States through bloodshed. There were the American Indian wars, the wars with Mexico and with Spain, and the Civil War, all wars that resulted in new citizens, America's minorities (the Asian American the exception here, historically, though there was the 1880 rebellion in Hawaii, America's entry into the 1900 Boxer Rebellion against China, and wars with Japan, Korea, Vietnam). There is the sense by those who are already structurally assimilated that those who enter the country voluntarily will make cultural adjustments, that they decided, implicitly, to assimilate.

The second factor affecting complete assimilation concerns concentration: how many are there? When the mode of entry is voluntary, the numbers entering tend not to be great enough to cause a threat to the majority. When the mode of entry is through conquest, the numbers of the conquered tend to be greater than the conquerors. Smaller numbers would more likely be absorbed (the American Indian no exception here, the majority once, subjected to genocide in the East, displacement in the West). But whether voluntarily or through conquest, sometimes the numbers coming in or trying to take part in overall social and economic structures appear too great. When that happens, race enters as a major factor. Sometimes the "race" is created, as in the case of the New Immigrants from Southern and Eastern Europe in the early 1900s, essentially white people who took on a hue: olive-skinned or somehow ruddy; or as in the case of Mexicans, who were also migrating to the United States in substantial numbers at the same time as the New Immigrants: very often racially white, rendered brown. Numbers get solved by way of race.

So the third element: race. Race becomes a factor when numbers become a problem. That is, race and the resulting definition of a cultural group as inferior come into play when the majority find the numbers of the new group threatening. The numbers of that threatening cultural group then become legally controlled. Case in point: the institution of quotas for those who would be called "the New Immigrants," those from Eastern Europe and the Mediterranean basin attempting entry.

With the New Immigrants, race was virtually anthropologically constructed. Consider the findings of anthropologist Madison Grant, an authority cited in a critical 1911 report to President Theodore Roosevelt on the immigration problem:

> The new immigration contained a large and increasing number of the weak, the broken, and the mentally crippled of all races drawn from the lowest stratum of the Mediterranean basin and the Balkans, together with hordes of the wretched, submerged populations of the Polish ghettoes. Our jails, insane asylums, and almshouses are filled with human flotsam and the whole tone of American life, social, moral, and political, has been lowered and vulgarized by them (Estrada et al., 115).

With the help of this report, legal restrictions against the admission of ruddy-skinned Eastern European and olive-skinned Mediterranean New Immigrants to the United States were instituted in 1924.

One more case in point: the 1928 congressional hearings on Western Hemisphere Immigration. The "race" (not really a single race at all, though treated monolithically): Mexicans. A number of speakers before the hearings put forth a concerted effort to stop the flow of Mexican migrants. According to one speaker,

> [Mexicans'] minds run to nothing higher than animal functions—eat, sleep, and sexual debauchery. In every huddle of Mexican shacks one meets the same idleness, hordes of hungry dogs, and filthy children with faces plastered with flies, disease, lice, human filth, stench, promiscuous fornication, bastardly, lounging, apathetic peons and lazy squaws, beans and

> dried fruit, liquor, general squalor, and envy and hatred of the gringo. These people sleep by day and prowl by night like coyotes, stealing anything they can get their hands on, no matter how useless to them it may be. Nothing left outside is safe unless padlocked or chained down. Yet there are Americans clamoring for more of these human swine to be brought over from Mexico (Estrada et al., 116).

The attempt failed—until the Great Depression. Then the numbers of Mexicans were lowered by way of forced expatriation. Mexicans and Mexican Americans who applied for relief were directed to "Mexican Bureaus." But rather than receive aid, the Mexicans were packed into cattle cars and railroaded to a Mexico that for many had never been their home (Estrada et al., 117). In 1933 a Los Angeles eyewitness to the expatriation process expressed the common sentiment:

> The repatriation programme is regarded locally as a piece of consummate statecraft. The average per family cost of executing it is $71.14, including food and transportation. It cost one Los Angeles County $77,249.29 to repatriate one shipment of 6,024. It would have cost $424,933.70 to provide this number with such charitable assistance as they would have been entitled to had they remained—a savings of $347,468.40 (Estrada et al., 118).

From 1929-1934 the number of repatriated Mexicans exceeded 400,000. Approximately half were native to the United States.

Other cases in point: the Chinese Exclusion Act of 1882, the denial of statehood for Arizona—twice—because of the territory's "mongrel racial character," the forced removal of American Indian children from their families and cultural ways, the denial of plebiscite proceedings for Puerto Rico, in part because of its having declared Spanish as equal with English, the many states enacting English-only laws (Baver; Conklin and Lourie; Daniels; Estrada et al.; K. Jensen). Cases are many.

And what the cases tell is of racism arising out of a colonial mentality, a colonial sensibility, in which the dominant culture fears the nonselective influence of other cultures on its own (as opposed to the selective influence of Mexican food on U.S. culture, say). British sociologist John Rex states flatly: "Racial discrimination and racial prejudice are phenomena of colonialism" (75).

Colonialism and Race

A colonial past may not be all there is to racism, but no other theory has the explanatory power of colonization theory—not theories of biological deficiency nor cultural deficiency nor racial inequality. Biological deficiency theories no longer gather large followings. Few today would listen to the likes of the nineteenth-century Harvard naturalist Louis Agassiz, who claimed that the brain of the Negro adult "never gets beyond that observable in the Caucasian in boyhood" (Franklin, 3). Still, Arthur Jensen could argue, in 1969, that African Americans are genetically inferior to Whites—and have his ideas published in distinguished journals like the *Harvard Education Review* and in popular magazines like *Psychology Today*. And the popular press was given to making public the Rutgers University "findings" that African Americans are genetically relegated to the low ends of the academic bell curve. Biological determinacy remains, despite seeming so obviously untenable.

Cultural counters to biological deficiency theories are not much better. In Thomas Farrell's version of cultural deficit theory, for example, it is suggested that African Americans suffer a cognitive disadvantage because they reside in an oral culture. His oral-culture hypothesis appeared in 1983, part of a trend, really. Sixteen years earlier, in 1967, Frantz Fanon wrote:

> The Negro loves to jabber [says contemporary psychoanalytic theory], and from this theory it is not a long road that leads to a proposition: The Negro is just a child. The psychoanalysts have a fine start here, and the term *orality* is soon heard (27, his italics).

Fanon's criticism combines the biological with the cultural to demonstrate the ways in which "science" retains racial biases. Neither theoretical method is viable.

Racial inequality theories, on the other hand, do have merit. Educational anthropologist John Ogbu presents a three-tiered minority hierarchy in America to explain racial inequality: caste-like minorities at bottom, followed by autonomous minorities, followed by immigrant minorities. The idea of an immigrant minority, to take them in reverse order, is clear. Even if the immigrant group maintains its ethnicity—like, say, Italians often do—the qualities ascribed that ethnicity are not such that the immigrant group would be necessarily excluded from the mainstream. The autonomous are those who maintain their cultural or religious distinctiveness yet manage to accommodate the mainstream, even if not assimilate. Ogbu cites American Jews and Mormons as instances of autonomous minorities. The caste-like are those who are regarded primarily on the basis of some particular birth ascription, in this country, a particular race or a particular ethnicity, race and ethnicity often being confused in America. Caste-like minorities cannot transcend their race or ethnicity.

For all their worth, however, racial inequality theories have a historical shortcoming. The ideology of racial difference is relatively new. Barrera traces it to the eighteenth century. Michael Banton traces the first published consideration of race relations, as such, to 1850. Prior to the eighteenth century, supposed cultural inferiority or religious inferiority of some races determined their suitability for slavery or other forms of oppression. So there is something older at work than racism, as we have come to understand it. Racial inequality theory does not explain, for example, why East Indians are considered black by the British but not by Americans. The most suggestive answer is, of course, that India was a British colony, not an American colony. The American East Indian is more often just another foreigner, another immigrant. Race alone is not the distinctive factor. Race, culture, and entry by way of imperial conquest make for the caste-like minority.

Colonization theory refines the concept of the caste-like minority by looking to the common feature in the caste-like's histories—colonization or the colonial-like. The autonomous minority holds no memory of colonization in this country. The majority holds no memory of having subjugated the autonomous minority or the immigrant for any length of time, nothing like the century of rule over the Puerto Rican, the century over the Mexican, centuries over the American Indian, the entire history of the African American, the Asian (the Asian mainly by way of its Pacific Island colonies). Looking to colonization makes a distinction not contained in race alone.

But what of race? What of the objections raised a quarter century ago about equating the African-American historical and social-political situation with colonization? The problem some social scientists had with equating African-American oppression with colonization was that whereas colonization was more a matter of land and resources than people (except when the people could be used to work the land and the resources), there was no African-American land in the United States. Social scientists noted, quite rightly, that African Americans were not the indigenous majority being ruled by a foreign minority. But the lack of a one-to-one correspondence between the history of colonialism and the history of American slavery does not negate the essential parallels.

American slavery and global classical colonialism, worldwide expansion, occur during the same historical moment. Robert Blauner even suggests that the slave trade of the late seventeenth and eighteenth centuries might have made the various indigenous peoples of Africa susceptible to their colonization, given the exposure to the European and given the removal of some of Africa's healthiest, sturdiest people. Blauner goes on to argue that slavery made possible the growth of America's textile industry, an industry which was critical to America's economic ascendancy within the Western world. And with the ascendancy and the expansion came the sense of cultural and racial superiority which continues to justify the exploitation of the culturally and racially "other." Despite surface differences between colonialism and slavery, they are essentially the same. In Blauner's words,

> The essential condition for both American slavery and European colonialism was the power domination and the technological superiority of the Western world in its relation

> to the peoples of non-Western and non-white origins. This objective supremacy in technology and military power buttressed the West's sense of cultural superiority, laying the basis for racist ideologies that were elaborated to justify control and exploitation of non-white people. Thus because classical colonialism and America's internal versions developed out of a similar balance of technological, cultural, and power relations, a common *process* of social oppression characterized the racial patterns in the two contexts—despite the variation in political and social structure (178-79).

Similarities between the American slave trade and European colonialism supersede differences.

One more major contention remains. And that is that the colonization process includes the deterioration of the cultures and traditions of the colonized. This process, say those who resist equating the African-American experience with internal colonialism, would not be the case for the African American, since the African American—as distinguished from Black Africans—never had a culture radically different from White Americans. Philip Curtin, for instance, in contrasting Black Africans with African Americans, writes that for African Americans, "[t]he prolonged separation from their African roots caused Afro-Americans to become thoroughly Western in all aspects of their culture. The strains in New World societies were therefore primarily between racial groups with only minor cultural differences" (25). African Americans suffer racism, plain and simple, say Curtin and others.

Blauner's response to the deculturation-en route argument is that America wrote the book on this aspect of the colonization process. "America's internal colonization," he writes, "has been more extreme than situations of classic colonialism" (183).

While scholars like Altbach and Kelly or Curtin will concede a definition of internal colonialism that circumvents boundary distinctions, defining "nation" as a distinct cultural group, they will not allow African Americans that distinction. Yet Fanon, especially in *Black Skin, White Masks*, describes the process whereby the colonizing ideology which strips a people of its culture becomes a process of creating a new culture, particularly when race is a factor. His term is "negritude." Negritude is the process whereby the colonized—Black, humiliated, ashamed of his race, alienated—in the process of disalienation comes to take pride in what had been the cause of his humiliation. This, according to Fanon, is the beginning of a dialectical process that leads to a recovery or realization of the colonized's humanity. What Fanon describes is a process with remarkable similarities to Signithia Fordham's fictive-kinship relationships. This is how she describes the historical formation of the fictive-kinship system:

> [T]he system was developed partly in response to two types of mistreatment from Whites: the economic and instrumental exploitation by Whites during and after slavery, and the historical and continuing tendency by White Americans to treat Black Americans as an undifferentiated mass of people, indiscriminately ascribing to them certain inherent strengths and weaknesses.... Black Americans have generally responded to this mistreatment by inverting the negative stereotypes and assumptions of Whites into positive and functional attributes.... Thus, Black Americans may have transformed White people's assumptions of Black homogeneity into a collective identity system (56-57).

"If there is an inferiority complex [within the Black colonized]," writes Fanon, "it is the outcome of a double process:—primarily economic;—subsequently, the internalization—or, better, the epidermalization—of this inferiority" (13)—and its solution begins with negritude, the creation of fictive-kinship relationships.

My contention, then, is this: African Americans were historically colonized, in the very deepest sense of having been removed from their lands, religions, languages—their cultures. As a result of the unrelenting ideology of colonization—the denial of a cultural identity and the concomitant denial of an identity with—and a denial of full access to—the society of the colonizer, the African American created a new ethnicity, a culture distinct from various Black Africans, distinct from White Americans in important ways, including dialect, a kind of language. African Americans are the internally colonized, no less than America's other ethnic-others, minorities, people of color, those whose histories are uncontestedly of colonization (especially American Indians and Latinos), those whose experiences continue to be the psychological, political, economic, social, and educational experiences of the colonized.

Education, Literacy, and Language

The schools of the colony contain curricula that aim at cultural assimilation, a limited assimilation, an assimilation that best serves the needs of those who hold power. An example comes from Kelly in relation to the Vietnamese under French rule. In the search for something like a multiculturalism, the French taught Vietnamese culture to the Vietnamese—in French. But since, to use Fanon's words, "[t]o speak a language is to take on a world, a culture" (38), the Vietnamese children found themselves ostensibly without a world or a culture: somehow distanced from their original cultural ways and somehow kept at a distance from the colonizers'.

In our own country, we have the example of Richard Rodriguez, the story of his education told in *Hunger of Memory* (1982). Rodriguez's intent, evidently, is to argue the case for assimilation by way of his own successful assimilation. Yet there is a tension throughout his book: the loss of his first cultural ways—and his ultimate failure at full assimilation. Rodriguez remains, after all, the Mexican American—in his being anthologized, in his being interviewed, in his overall notoriety. His ethnicity remains ever present: a credit to his people, the model for Mexican Americans, according to Anglo-American critics; a traitor to his people, according to his Latino critics. Culturally, he reflects the insufficiency of an assimilationist model (even as he espouses assimilation), even if economically, perhaps, he has achieved some success.

Economic comfort is not all there is. There will always be those who will attain it. It is a commonplace, recognizable to all, that the numbers are never equitable, the percentage of people of color who achieve a kind of economic success, a middle class, maybe more, is never on a par with those who are not people of color. And this, too, is within the colonial frame. Altbach and Kelly write of the two great reasons for the colonized's acceptance of colonial education: economic ascension and cultural resignation. In their words:

> While economic self-betterment was the major motif in the colonized's acceptance of colonial schools, it was not the only reason why, by the end of the nineteenth century, the colonized flocked to the schools. In colonies where nation-states had preceded foreign domination, nationalism figured prominently in many parents' decisions to send their children to colonial schools. The fact of foreign rule and its seeming permanence shook the faith of many of the indigenous people in the viability of their culture and institutions as they were. Learning Western technology and science seemed the key to revitalization of their own societies and their return to autonomy (17).

Replace "Western" with "White," "nationalism" with "equity" or even "complete structural assimilation," and the analogy becomes apparent. Cultural integrity, something greater than mere racial tolerance, and the possibility for "economic self-betterment" must become realized through the schools.

Though I believe that integrity and parity for all is already the desire of educators generally, I don't believe that the way to making that desire a reality has been found. Take, for example, our ways with literacy instruction. In the later 1960s, William Labov popularized the realization that the language of African American people was not just slang nor a subdialect. The language of African Americans of the inner city is a bona fide dialect, a variation of English that is rule-governed, consistent, with unique historical precedents, linked to West African languages and the English of mainly Irish plantation taskmasters, no more "sub" than the English of Boston. What followed was an aim at not disparaging a student's dialect. But that posed problems, since most teachers did not speak that dialect (teachers tending not to be from among the colonized), since higher education and the market required another dialect, a requirement not likely to change, whatever the pronouncement of linguists. The student's right to her own dialect was an admirable sentiment, but not practical, sighed those who understood the integrity of a culture's ways with words.

The student's right to her own dialect has since been replaced by the student's right to her own voice. The result has been a greater acceptance of narrative writing, whether written by students or written by scholars, promoted from scholars who attempt to be relatively neutral politically to those who are more radical. There is a voice of consensus over the need to have students discover their own voices—at least among literacy specialists. That voice, however, is to find expression through Standard American English. The marketplace still requires "correct English"—that is, the standard dialect, the dialect of those who have traditionally received prestige. The University still requires "academic discourse," essentially the same prestige dialect as the standard. So the contradiction: students' own voice is to be voiced in mandated ways. Even the forward-thinking "voice advocates" continue to require linguistic or rhetorical monoculturalism.

A multicultural acceptance of voice would acknowledge different cultures' different ways with discourse, different rhetorics, thereby leaving the long colonial trail. The Latino's or Latina's ways with discourse, for example, follow a colonial trail that finds its origins in the Greece of the fifth century BCE (Before the Common Era) and ends with a commonality with the discursive ways of present-day Arab speakers and writers (Ostler). Arabs were the colonial rulers of Spain for seven hundred years, ousted from Spain the same year that Columbus set sail to the New World. Before that, there were Arabs who lived in what is now Turkey—Rhomaic Arabs, collaborators with the rulers of the Byzantine Empire, speakers of Greek. The Byzantine Empire's ways with words were Greek, with the rhetorical manner known as sophistry. Byzantium had also ruled Spain. The first ruler of Byzantium, Constantine, had been ruler of Rome. Rome's cultural teachers were the Greeks. The sophists sold their rhetorical ways to Greece, though their place of origin tended to be Italy. Italy had also once ruled Spain. And at the time of the first flourishing of sophistry, parts of Italy were colonies of Greece, of the city-state of Athens (Villanueva, "Hispanic/Latino Writing"). One colonial ruler of Spain after another for over two thousand years was given to sophistry, the traces of the sophistic remaining among the descendants of Spain.

How all this takes shape, even among Latinos and Latinas who are monolingual in English, is in a discourse which tends to stylistic repetition at the word level, the sentence level, the discourse level. The Latino or Latina writer is also given to the metaphorical, the poetic, the florid. And he or she is given to a kind of alinearity, seeming digressions from the line of logic with which to underscore an argument (Villanueva, "Hispanic"). A multicultural perspective that would at least acknowledge these and other culturally determined rhetorical devices would provide for the possibility of a new way of seeing multicultural literacy instruction, a perspective that would break from a too long-standing colonial tradition.

What tends to take place, however, is that the very patterns of discourse—the manifestations of logic—demanded by the schools become imposed on all the cultures within the schools. When it comes to language and language instruction, this has been the traditional way with the colonized. Say Altbach and Kelly in reference to neocolonialism, for example:

> The question of language is a key element of the neocolonial relationship.... [T]he colonizers often imposed their language on their colonies and used this language for important societal functions. Typically, the legal system, most of the educational system, most governmental functions, and the commercial spheres tied to the colonial power were conducted in a European language. Over time the European

> language became *the* language for "modern" communication, with the bulk of newspapers, journals, books, and serious discussion taking place in this language (37).

This describes what we now term "Global English"—a phenomenon of which we Americans tend to be proud, but a reflection of where the global metropole can be found, of the colonial center, debtor nation notwithstanding. Whatever each of our personal views on contemporary American empire, Americans of color should hold greater than Third-World status within our own country.

So what to do? Here this essay runs out. My interest has been in pointing to a problem and opening discussion on possible solutions. Our best efforts at this point have been to turn to Paulo Freire's theory of a critical consciousness. This is an honorable turn. I can think of none better as I write, have thought of none better as I have taught. It best serves the needs of multiculturalism in exposing the degree to which the multicultural finds resistance in entrenched caricatures of difference, facile stereotypes, rather than in a bona fide politics of difference, in which there is a constant dialectical interplay between the things we all have in common and our cultural and historical differences.

In critical consciousness is the recognition that society contains social, political, and economic conditions which are at odds with the individual will to freedom. When that recognition is given voice and a decision is made to do something about the contradiction between the individual and the society's workings against individual freedom, there is *praxis*. Freire would have students look at their individual histories and cultures and compare those histories and ways of being with what they are led to believe is their place in the world, making the contradictions between their worldviews and official worldviews explicit. Simply knowing is a kind of power. And being able to give voice to that knowledge without having to repress culturally determined ways with discourse gives credence to our acceptance of that power, provides for a new, stronger multiculturalism.

A powerful multiculturalism remains as the overall goal of most of us: the cultural and historical affirmations among all of

America's citizens, both from people of color and from America's descendants of immigrants. But we can't arrive at the goal as long as we continue to follow an assimilationist model, since with an assimilationist model those who will be most affected negatively will be America's people of color. Critical consciousness, a critical appraisal of the contradictions people of color in particular contain as members of often antagonistic cultures, might make for a conscious decision to accommodate the demands of the larger culture while seeking to make that larger culture more inclusive.

Bibliography

Altbach, Philip G., and Gail P. Kelly. *Education and Colonialism*. New York: Longman, 1978.

Banton, Michael. "1960: A Turning Point in the Study of Race Relations." In *Slavery, Colonialism, and Racism*, edited by Sidney W. Mintz. New York: Norton, 1974.

Barrera, Mario. *Race and Class in the Southwest: A Theory of Racial Inequality*. Notre Dame, IN: University of Notre Dame Press, 1979.

Baver, Sherrie L. *The Political Economy of Colonialism: The State and Industrialization in Puerto Rico*. Westport, CT: Praeger, 1993.

Blauner, Robert. "Internal Colonialism and Ghetto Revolt." In *Social Reality*, edited by Harvey A. Farberman and Erich Goode. Englewood Cliffs, NJ: Prentice-Hall, 1973.

Carmichael, Stokely, and Charles Hamilton. *Black Power*. New York: Random House, 1967.

Clark, Kenneth. *Dark Ghetto*. New York: Harper and Row, 1965.

Conklin, Nancy Faires, and Margaret A. Lourie. *A Host of Tongues: Language Communities in the United States*. New York: The Free Press, 1983.

Cose, Ellis. *The Rage of a Privileged Class*. New York: HarperCollins, 1993.

Cruse, Harold. *Rebellion or Revolution*. New York: Morrow, 1968.

Curtin, Philip D. "The Black Experience of Colonialism and Imperialism." In *Slavery, Colonialism, and Racism*, edited by Sidney W. Mintz. New York: Norton, 1974.

Daniels, Harvey, ed. *Not Only English: Affirming America's Multilingual Heritage*. Urbana, IL: NCTE, 1990.

Estrada, Leonardo F., F. Chris Garcia, Reynaldo Flores Macias, and Lionel Maldonado. "Chicanos in the United States: A History of Exploitation and Resistance." *Daedalus* 2 (1981): 103-31.

Fanon, Frantz. *Black Skin, White Masks*. Translated by Charles Lam Markmann. New York: Grove, 1967.

Farrell, Thomas J. "IQ and Standard English." *College Composition and Communication* 34 (1983): 470-84.

Fordham, Signithia. "Racelessness as a Factor in Black Students' School Success: Pragmatic Strategy or Pyrrhic Victory? *Harvard Education Review* 58 (1988): 54-84.

Frank, Andre Gunder. *Capitalism and Underdevelopment in Latin America*. New York: Monthly Review, 1967.

Franklin, John Hope. "The Land of Room Enough." *Daedalus* 110 (1981): 1-12.

Fraser, Cary. *Ambivalent Anti-Colonialism: The United States and the Genesis of West Indian Independence, 1940-1964*. Westport, CT: Greenwood, 1994.

Freire, Paulo. *Pedagogy of the Oppressed*. Translated by Myra Bergman Ramos. New York: Herder and Herder, 1970.

Gramsci, Antonio. *Selections from the Prison Notebooks*. Edited and translated by Quiten Hoare and Geoffrey Nowell Smith. New York: International, 1971.

———. "The Southern Question." In *The Modern Prince and Other Writings*. Translated by Louis Marks. New York: International, 1957.

Hechter, Michael. *Internal Colonialism: The Celtic Fringe in British National Development, 1536-1966*. Berkeley: University of California Press, 1975.

Jensen, Arthur R. "The Differences Are Real." *Psychology Today* 7 (1973): 80-82, 84, 86.

———. "How Much Can We Boost IQ and Scholastic Achievement?" *Harvard Education Review* 39 (1969): 1-123.

Jensen, Katherine. "Civilization and Assimilation in the Colonized Schooling of Native Americans." In *Education and the Colonial Experience*, edited by Philip G. Altbach and Gail P. Kelly. New Brunswick, NJ: Transaction, 1984.

Kelly, Gail P. "Colonialism, Indigenous Society, and School Practices: French West Africa and Indochina, 1918-1938." In *Education and the Colonial Experience*, edited by Philip G. Altbach and Gail P. Kelly. New Brunswick, NJ: Transaction, 1984.

Ogbu, John U. *Minority Education and Caste: The American System in Cross-Cultural Perspective*. New York: Academic, 1978.

Ostler, Shirley E. "English in Parallels: A Comparison of English and Arabic Prose." *Writing across Languages: Analysis of L2 Text*. Eds. Ulla Connor and Robert B. Kaplan. Reading, MA: Addison-Wesley, 1987.

Rex, John. *Race, Colonialism and the City*. London: Routledge and K. Paul, 1973.

Rodriguez, Richard. *Hunger of Memory: The Education of Richard Rodriguez*. New York: Bantam, 1982.

Ross, Robert J. S., and Kent C. Trachte. *Global Capitalism: The New Leviathan*. Albany: SUNY, 1990.

Villanueva, Victor, Jr. *Bootstraps: From an American Academic of Color*. Urbana, IL: NCTE, 1993.

———. "Hispanic/Latino Writing: Rhetorical Differences." *Encyclopedia of English Studies and Language Arts*, edited by Alan C. Purves. Urbana, IL: NCTE, in press.

———. "On Writing Groups, Class, and Culture: Studying Oral and Literate Language Features." *Writing With: New Directions in Collaborative Teaching, Learning, and Research*, edited by Sally Barr Reagan, Thomas Fox, and David Bleich. New York: SUNY Press, 1994.

Wallerstein, Immanuel. *The Capitalist World Economy*. Cambridge: Cambridge University Press, 1979.

Chapter 5

The Mulatto in American Literature

W. Maurice Shipley

> ...the...world...has given color meaning and color becomes the most distinguishing factor of your existence.
>
> —H. Rap Brown

If one accepts that color is "...the most distinguishing factor..." of one's existence, then Dennis Fischman's study ("Getting It: Multiculturalism and the Politics of Understanding") makes a tragic commentary on this country's failure to make substantive growth in understanding racial differences. Three decades have passed since the volatile, race-conscious '60s, yet the problems that Americans face with multiculturalism make a poignant statement about our lack of growth. We "...just don't get it."[1] What exactly does it take to elicit empathy without sympathy? After all, no culture wants the inaction which is the result of sympathy. Rather, one hopes for the action that accompanies empathy. And while I am inclined to agree with Fischman, when he concludes that a group can "...rightfully demand empathy the way it demands justice,"[2] I fully understand that empathy does not necessarily lead to "justice"—surely not legislative.

This study is based on the premise that color not only distinguishes our existence but, in many ways, informs the development of our arts and social institutions. And, if it is true, as stated by the poet Shelley that: "Poets are the unacknowledged legislators of the world,"[3] then a study of ethnic literature may well offer one a key to cultural understanding.

More specifically, this study contends that by looking at the image of the mulatto, as it has been developed throughout much of American literature and culture, one not only sees possibilities presented by intercultural melding but better understands much of what needs to be overcome.

Any study which focuses on the mulatto or the "image" of the mulatto in American literature must necessarily consider political history as well as literary history. For the mulatto in America has long been an enigma. Even today, the questions of racial identity and how best to cope with issues of miscegenation (past and present) raise concerns which have, historically, been difficult for Americans.

In his treatise on race relations in America, Winthrop Jordan makes some very interesting observations regarding the word "mulatto" and its historical derivations. Unlike the dictionary, which defines mulatto as the "first generation offspring of a pure Negro and a white," Jordan notes: "The word 'mulatto' is not frequently used in the United States. It is customarily reserved for biological contexts, and for social purposes a mulatto is termed a Negro."[4]

For all practical purposes, Jordan was saying that whites in America have taken a rather simplistic approach as to how they have historically dealt with mulattoes. All that was needed was to rely on the dictionary to speak to the biological question while defining mulattoes as Black in all things social. This, in effect, would make allowances for applying to them the same laws regarding Blacks. It would also eliminate the need to confront one of the realities of America's slave history.

The word "mulatto" is derived from the Spanish. Jordan notes that it came into English usage around 1600. Problems were immediate. How was this mulatto individual to be treated? Was he Black or white? What laws were applicable to him or her? Would not the product of miscegenation serve to raise questions in regard to Southern mores and morality? Were not mulattoes a genuine threat to either an erosion or total collapse of the existing rules of separation of the races? Would the United States develop a caste system, such as existed in the Caribbean? The questions were many, and answers were desperately needed. To be sure, the central issues were politically and sociologically motivated.

The subject of miscegenation was one which the South, historically, had sought to ignore—even hide, when it was blatantly obvious to everyone that it was a common practice. Quoting pioneer sociologist E. B. Reuter, George Fredrickson states: "Miscegenation is likely to be especially extensive where the predominant relationship is between master and slave, because slaveholders have easy access to the women of the servile class."[5] Clearly, the existence of slavery presupposed miscegenation.

In an attempt to dissuade whites from either cohabiting with slaves or being intimate with them, there was a need for laws. Even so, the widespread practice virtually insured the failure of any legal "solution."

Reuter deduced that: "...a dominant group can prescribe three possible positions for "half-castes": they may be the lower segment of the dominant group; members of the exploited group; or an intermediate class or caste."[6] The "choice" was not difficult. To make mulattoes a "lower segment" of white culture would admit the fact of miscegenation and make allowances for their ancestry. That could create unique problems in both social interaction and the legal arena. Creation of an intermediate group meant a caste system, which would mitigate against the politics of slavery. The only solution was to make them a part of the "exploited group" (that is, they were considered Black).

Virginia led the way in the creation of laws to inhibit miscegenation. In 1662, a law was passed, doubling the fine for "interracial fornicators."[7] Fredrickson refers to this as "...the first clearcut example of statutory racial discrimination in American history."[8] Shortly thereafter (1664), Maryland passed a law forbidding interracial marriage—stating that if a white woman were to marry a slave, she would virtually become a slave herself for the lifetime of her husband. In 1691, Virginia passed another law, which essentially forbade all interracial marriages. The law was careful to include mulattoes. Ultimately, "by the middle of the

18th century, six of the thirteen colonies had made interracial marriage punishable by laws."[9] John Hope Franklin put the figure for mulattoes (who were slaves) at 246,000 out of a total slave population of 3.2 million. He further noted that the number was probably considerably higher, but only those mulattoes who appeared to be obviously mulattoes counted.

The fact is that miscegenation had become commonplace. Not only did servitude perpetuate it, but a growing perversion of sexual attitudes and mores conspired to make it even more difficult to legislate against. In his book *Roll Jordan Roll: The World the Slaves Made*, Eugene Genovese notes that 13 percent of the Black American population in 1860 had white ancestry.[10] Genovese goes on to say that by 1850, 37 percent of the free Black population in the United States was part white and that the figure was much higher for the free Black population living in the South.[11]

The fact that miscegenation was such a firmly entrenched aspect of slavery somewhat simplifies historical realities. For many years, Black females outnumbered Black males. And white males outnumbered white females.

Moreover, the fact that no caste system existed mitigated against consistency in the treatment of mulattoes. Many suffered jealousy and hatred from both groups. Sure, some went to work at the "big house" and had the "opportunity" to (sometimes) keep their children with them. But they were few. More often than not, mulattoes suffered extremely harsh treatment. They were anomalies, and white America did not know how to deal with them.

To whites, mulattoes represented a very real confrontation with reality. Mulattoes represented to both Blacks and whites reminders of flagrant sexual abuse and perverted desires. Finally, for Blacks, mulattoes represented a total disrespect for Black womanhood and Black values. The abuse was exacerbated by the fact that children born of the abuse were essentially forced to forget the realities of their history and to accept a distorted reality—that they were not different from other blacks. It was a convenient method of denying miscegenation.

A caste system could work in the Caribbean, because whites constituted a small portion of the population.[12] Consequently, whites encouraged the growth of a caste system so as to enable them to build a buffer between themselves and Blacks. Mulattoes were encouraged to become tradesmen, managers, and small proprietors. Such was not the case in the American South where whites were a much larger proportion of the population. Mulattoes were Black, and Blacks were slaves. There were no allowances for other aspirations—outside the life of a slave.

Indeed, as early as the 1730s, the "...Jamaican legislature gave mulattoes unique rights (over Blacks)—to inherit planters' plantations."[13]

The mulatto in American literature has been a unique vehicle from the inception of the image in the literature. Positioned between two cultures, unsure of how to embrace either, the mulatto character in American literature afforded white (and Black) writers a myriad of opportunities to safely explore areas of which they had only imagined. White writers could use them for propaganda and to espouse the evils of miscegenation, while Black writers could use them to point out the many tragedies and other ramifications of slavery. For many writers who utilized the (mulatto) character in their works, prior to the abolition of slavery, the mulatto could either be used to espouse antislavery sentiment or for overt propaganda supporting the most racist philosophy.

Judith Berzon points out that "the mulatto has captured the imaginations of American novelists writing during every period of literature."[14] She includes a list of writers ranging from: Mark Twain, William Faulkner, Sinclair Lewis, and Willa Cather to Harriet Beecher Stowe, William Wells Brown, Charles W. Chestnutt, James W. Johnson, and Nella Larsen. Berzon's list is not intended to be all-inclusive, rather, to illustrate a range in culture, gender, notoriety, and time periods.

In either case, there was a conscientious positing of racial stereotypes and myths that, over a considerable period of time, would mitigate against a very ordered development in American literature — especially Black American literature. Berzon observes that between 1844 and 1865, the mulatto character became a central figure in American literature.[15] This interest or fascination with the mulatto character may well be viewed as a direct by-product of an overall interest of Southern writers in Blacks generally. Albion Tourgee observed:

> A foreigner studying our current literature without knowledge of our history and judging our civilization by our fiction, would undoubtedly conclude that the South was the seat of intellectual empire in America, and the African the chief romantic element of our civilization.[16]

The interest in Blacks and mulattoes as a focus for literary themes extended beyond Southern boundaries as novelists, dramatists, poets, and short-story writers in a myriad of cultures progressively came to realize the extent to which they could utilize the characters in order to examine deeper philosophical and sociological issues.

Much of the early literature focusing on the mulatto was antislavery literature. It developed the stereotype of the "tragic mulatto." This was the image of the mulatto as stranded, pathetically, between two races—a victim of racial limbo or doomed to a sad end. In the words of Arthur P. Davis:

> The tragic mulatto stereotype stemmed from the antislavery crusade, whose authors used it, partly to show miscegenation as an evil of slavery, partly as an attempt to win readers' sympathies by presenting central characters who were physically very like the readers. Antislavery authors...held to a crude kind of racism. Their near-white characters are the intransigent, the resentful, the mentally alert—for biological, not social reasons. In the proslavery argument, the mixed blood characters are victims of a divided inheritance and proof of the disastrous results of amalgamation. Most of the villains in reconstruction fiction are mixed bloods.[17]

The stereotype of the tragic mulatto became a favorite of both Black and white writers regardless of locale. Indeed, this stereotype has persisted longer than most others—emerging out of slavery. Examples of such writers are: James W. Johnson, Nella Larsen, Kate Chopin, Gayl Jones, Alice Walker, Mari Evans, and John Updike.

From the turn of the century until the Harlem Renaissance, literature about mulattoes illustrated interesting contrasts between Black and white writers. In the works of most white writers, mulattoes were essentially destined for a sad end. In the works of most Black writers, mulattoes found themselves faced with the quandary of a race identity decision. This quandary is poignantly captured in the Langston Hughes' poem "Cross," when the mulatto sorrowfully states:

> My old man died in a fine big house.
> My ma died in a shack.
> I wonder where I'm gonna die,
> Being neither white nor black?[18]

Moreover, up until the Harlem Renaissance, the mulatto received similar treatment in the works of white male and female writers—in that sexuality often played an important role. For the white male writer, if the mulatto was a male, then he often sought out a white woman. If the character was a female, she somehow bedeviled and deceived her white paramour with her sexuality. In both instances, the mulatto, having his/her racial identity made known, very quickly either lost everything he/she had acquired or met a more ignoble end. This is vividly illustrated in the works of James Fenimore Cooper, Nathaniel Hawthorne, and William Faulkner.

In Cooper's *The Last of the Mohicans*, the two heroines in the novel are sisters, but they have different mothers. Cora is a mulatto. Her sister, Alice, is not "tainted" by the mixture in Cora. Indeed, Alice is described as possessing a "...dazzling complexion, fair golden hair, and bright blue eyes...."[19] Conversely, Cora, who is rarely described as thoroughly, is constantly spoken of as possessing a "dark eye" and having a bedeviling influence on the men, both white and Indian. She has the "misfortune" of having mixed blood, thereby negating any possible union between her and the white colonel Heyward. Her appeal and attractiveness are manifested primarily in Indian circles, not white. Even

Chingachgook and Leatherstocking voice their contempt for mixed-blood tribes. Ultimately, Cora meets a traditionally tragic end, thus fulfilling the theme of the "tragic mulatto." Any happy ending would only affirm miscegenation, to which Cooper was firmly opposed. His use of the mulatto helped to promote his philosophy of "stratification of the races." Cooper's novel is all the more significant when one understands that the focus on the mulatto theme was clearly crafted for his major audience—women—given that they were the principal readers of fiction at that time. This does not negate the action of the novel, which was geared to the male audience. It does point up conflicting significance. One would tend to think that Cooper was very cognizant of the fact that his theory on stratification of the races would find appeal with both women (who comprised his basic audience) and the general male audience.

For Nathaniel Hawthorne, the mulatto image had more power in suggestion, rather than in explicit statement. Moreover, Hawthorne realized that, utilized effectively, the image would allow him to enhance both the structure and plot of the novel. Consequently, Hawthorne used the image not only to enhance the mystery, but expand the parameters of *The Last of the Mohicans*.

Hawthorne suggests that one of his central protagonists, Miriam, was a mulatto—born the "offspring of a burning drop of African blood...."[20] When he suggested her possible mulatto heritage, Hawthorne was not simply recalling the history of Southern slavery, but was employing a mythological stereotype—suggesting that mixed blood somehow imbued one with mysterious and exotic qualities. This, somehow, "explains" both Miriam's strange beauty and a seemingly evil spirit which affects those closest to her. When she disappears at the end of the novel, the reader doesn't really question Hawthorne's plot development, especially when one realizes that he has been very consistent with the theme of the "tragic mulatto." Even Kenyon, her sculptor friend, refers to her disappearance as "cruelty."

William Faulkner is far more sophisticated in his use of the mulatto. This is due in large part to the fact that Faulkner was much more familiar with Black culture. Consequently, he was well versed with the various nuances of Black characters—especially mulattoes, as is exemplified in Faulkner's *Light in August*. At the same time, the novel makes a social commentary on the regional perspective of race and racial separation as manifested throughout history. This is well developed in the townspeople's attitude, as well as their perception of Joe Christmas. They see him as a mysterious enigma, someone to avoid. For Joanna Burden, he is a symbol of the South's slave history. As such, he represents one of the sins wrought by slavery—the rape of Black women. Joanna's sense of historical guilt is so oppressive that she reaches out to him for all the wrong reasons.

The central protagonist of *Light in August*, Joe Christmas, is a mulatto, whose relationship with white Joanna Burden is predicated on an earlier unexplained attraction which, the reader ultimately learns, is his mixed-blood heritage. This point is vividly illustrated during a sexual act when, in the throes of passion, she cries out "nigger, nigger." In linking Joe Christmas to a mysterious and sinister past and Joanna to Joe's negative history, Faulkner is able to use the mulatto image as a way of making a statement about the impact of slavery and Black people on the present.

When Joe Christmas meets his death, Faulkner cannot help making clear an attitude about miscegenation and race. The district attorney concludes that it is Joe Christmas's black blood which was his undoing because it "...failed him again, as it must have in crises all his life."[21] That conclusion in many ways makes clear exactly how the mixed-blood heritage of the mulatto has been utilized by a myriad of white American writers to advance philosophical and sociological ideologies, many of which mitigated against the best ideas of multiculturalism.

For white female writers, the mulatto was a character for compassion that, at times, bordered on complete pathos. There was a greater attempt to get the reader subjectively to approach the mulatto as a unique individual. Sexuality was not as much a focus as was the "deception" and the effect of that deception. Understanding why an individual of another race would choose to pass for white and the ramifications of such a decision on both the individual and those around him/her expanded the parameters of the basic plot and provided possibilities of a richer character development. For the most part, the mulatto fared somewhat better in the works of white women writers than in that of their male counterparts. Black female writers, such as Nella Larsen, employed the mulatto image as a way of making racial commentary on intraracial relationships and flawed value systems.

Black critics, such as Arthur Davis, observed that "...in books by white authors the whole desire of her (the mulatto, quadroon, or octoroon) is to find a white lover...."[22] Being thwarted by society, the mulattoes came to a tragic end. In looking at works by Black writers, Davis noted that they had "...turned the story around: now after restless searching, she finds peace only after returning to her own people."[23] In either case, Davis concludes that the mulatto suffers. But it is easy to view Davis's criticism as not wholly comprehensive in its scope.

For Black male writers, the mulatto was often politically aware and socially and personally deceptive in that his or her heritage precluded racial stereotyping and projected an aura of mystery. The male was not always some sexual brute who lusted after white women. More often than not, he was constantly struggling to come to terms with his racial ancestry—to find the inner calm which invariably came with the embracing of his Blackness. The character, even in deception, was often a good person, who simply wanted better.

Black women writers utilized the mulatto in a much more psychological way. The focus was on the inner machinations of decision making (on whether or not to "pass") and how to cope with what he/she was giving up. More often than not, sexuality was not a central part of the work. There was much more emphasis on the "secret" identity—whether it was secret or not. Often, the mulattoes found him-/herself drawn to other Blacks and had to struggle with an urge to allow themselves to feel strange yearnings.

In the last half century, mulatto literature has taken on a significant degree of diversity and sophistication. This is, in part, due to the political, social, and psychological development of Black culture. More important has been the emergence of writers, both Black and white, who are not only much more socially conscientious, but who do not necessarily find the mulatto a simplistic vehicle for propaganda or aesthetic literary messages. Contemporary writers who study the mulatto challenge themselves to find new ways to give the character literary substance. The challenge is to move beyond history and sociological simplicity—to find new ways of utilizing this most unique American and move him/her into the cultural mainstream.

Richard Wright once referred to the Negro as "America's metaphor." It would not be an overstatement to say that the mulatto is America's "anomaly." He/she has never quite fit in and has always been just a little out of place to both writers and to the mulattoes themselves—strangers in their own land. At the same time, the image begs for understanding, because it speaks to issues that separate races and people.

Another way of looking at the mulatto in American literature is to think of him/her as a unique ethnic, who happens to be a problem for Americans. In his classic study, *The Souls of Black Folks*, W.E.B. Du Bois observed that white Americans view Black people as a problem. Du Bois noted: "Between me and the other world there is ever an unasked question.... How does it feel to be a problem?"[24] Such is precisely the concern of the mulatto in both America and American literature. There is a direct correlation between unmeltable ethnics and mulattoes. It is reflected in the literature of American writers.

The mulattoes in American literature have consistently presented writers a problem. Are they Black or white? What of mulattoes who can pass as white? Were they not doubly dangerous? How could the individual be forced to accept a race which might want to deny his/her existence? What will be the political, sociological, and philosophical ramifications of embracing miscegenation? The best answers have all too often been to make the mulatto an outsider, a stranger in both worlds. In many ways, that is exactly what has happened to various ethnic groups in our society. Consequently, it is clear that the mulatto cannot be thought of as part of any one specific group even though society forces such individuals to embrace Black culture. In some states, there still exist laws which dictate the same. Even today, in some states, any portion of Black heritage dictates that the individual list him-/herself as Black.

The fact is that the mulatto character in American literature had been a pawn in our society's game of chess with its ethnic minorities and those for whom there exists a real quandary when it comes to compartmentalizing racial groups in order to keep them out of the cultural mainstream. This is, in effect, a blatant form of racism in that it stereotypes for the purpose of segregation and exclusion.

Perhaps one of the biggest concerns of American society today is how to infuse in the culture an acceptance of diversity and create a truly multicultural society. Reconciling the image of the mulatto in American literature with that goal is as perplexing today as it has been historically for American writers. Past history has not been a good teacher; recent history might lead to the kinds of results that change the future.

I must admit that discussions of multiculturalism and diversity cause me significant uneasiness because, as a Black man in America, I'd like to believe that my color has never been my problem. Inclusion has always been my goal—my dream. It seems to me that the same could be said of any ethnic group. For me, the question remains: how do I get America to accept my being different—especially when it seems to be no real comfort to understand the value in differences? Every time I have to explain that difference, I think to myself: "They still don't get it." And now, I wonder as I look over to my little mulatto grandson, whose smile is both my joy and my hope—how do I change his literature, his world, and make of it all that his smile thinks it is? He is right to say (and hope):

> I, too, sing America
> . . .
> Tomorrow,
> I'll be at the table
> . . .
> They'll see how beautiful I am
> And be ashamed—
> I, too, am America.
>
> —"I, Too" by Langston Hughes[25]

---

[1] Dennis Fischman, "Getting It: Multiculturalism and the Politics of Understanding." (See Table of Contents)

[2] Ibid., 19.

[3] Percy B. Shelley, *A Defence of Poetry and a Letter to the Lord Ellenbourg* (London: Porcupine Press, 1948), 54.

[4] Winthrop D. Jordan, *White over Black* (Chapel Hill, University of North Carolina Press, 1968), 167. [Jordan quotes a myriad of authorities in this treatise.]

[5] George Fredrickson, *White Supremacy* (New York, Oxford University Press, 1981), 101.

[6] Ibid.

[7] Ibid.

[8] Ibid.

[9] John Hope Franklin, *From Slavery to Freedom: A History of Negro Americans* (New York, Alfred A. Knopf, 1980), 55.

[10] Eugene Genovese, *Roll Jordan, Roll: The World the Slaves Made* (New York, Random House, 1976), 414.

[11] Ibid., 431.

[12] Jordan, *White over Black,* 10.

[13] Judith Berzon, *The Mulatto* (New York, University Press, 1978), 14.

[14] Ibid., 54.

[15] Ibid.

[16] Albion Tourgee, "The South As a Field for Fiction," *Forum* 6 (December 1988): 405.

[17] Sterling Brown, "A Century of Negro Portraiture in American Literature," in *Black Voices,* edited by Abraham Chapman (New York, New American Library, 1968).

[18] Langston Hughes in *Black Writers of America,* eds. Richard K. Barksdale and Kenneth Kinnaman (New York, Macmillan, 1972), 519.

[19] James Fenimore Cooper, *The Last of the Mohicans* (Boston, Riverside Press, 1958), 23.

[20] Nathaniel Hawthorne, *The Marble Faun* in *The Complete Novels and Selected Tales of Nathaniel Hawthorne,* ed. Norman Holmes Pearson (New York, Random House, 1937), 603.

[21] William Faulkner, *Light in August* (New York, Random House, 1968), 425.

[22] Sterling Brown, "Century of Negro Portraiture," 570

[23] Ibid., 571.

[24] W.E.B. Du Bois, *The Souls of Black Folks,* in *Three Negro Classics,* ed. John Hope Franklin (New York, Avon Books, 1965), 213.

[25] Barksdale and Kinnaman, *Black Writers of America,* 519.

Multicultural Dialogicalism: Personal Examples

Chapter 6

Representing and Negotiating Differences in the Contact Zone

Min-Zhan Lu

In an essay on multiculturalism in the academy, "Arts of the Contact Zone," Mary Louise Pratt defines the contact zone as a "social space where cultures meet, clash, and grapple with each other, often in contexts of highly asymmetrical relations of power, such as colonialism, slavery, or their aftermaths as they are lived out in many parts of the world today" (34). I am taken by the image of a "contact zone" because it foregrounds the necessary conflict and struggle involved in any attempt to achieve multiculturalism in the United States of today. However, learning to live cultural differences in a contact zone is challenging for all members of our society, those at the center as well as those on the margins, for it works against the grain of several common-sense views of diversity. When grasping one's relationship with diverse cultural sites, most of us tend to take an either/or approach: 1) we perceive cultures as discrete and self-contained rather than interactive and constructed in relation to others; 2) we perceive ourselves as strictly inside one and outside the rest of the cultures; 3) we view our cultural identity as strictly determined by such markers as place of birth, nationality, skin color, or other biological features; 4) we view issues of race, class, and gender as separate rather than intersecting. These prevalent approaches to diversity, working with a general emphasis on product over process, often lead us to "tour" cultures supposedly alien to those we consider our own. That is, our attempts at achieving multiculturalism tend to slide into a kind of "cultural tourism" in which we try to know more about diverse cultures by reading more texts written by and about people of diverse cultures without challenging the monocultural and, at times, even centrist point of view we habitually take toward these alien cultures. We assume that we are somehow outside of rather than implicated in the cultures *about* which we talk, read, and write; and we treat them as fixed and discrete entities or "things" to be recognized, grasped, and boiled down to bits of information which we can then in turn "have" and keep in our minds as souvenirs of our tour.

Let me use a personal story to explain my quarrel with cultural tourism as a method of living cultural difference. When I first arrived in this country, I took a bus tour through Harlem in New York City. At that time, for twenty-five dollars or so, you could take a bus tour to see all the attractions of New York City in one day. Harlem was listed as one of them, along with the Statue of Liberty, the United Nations building, and Chinatown. The only difference between visits to these latter attractions and the visit to Harlem was that when we got to Harlem, the bus drove straight through instead of stopping to allow us to get off and visit gift shops. After making sure that all the windows and doors on the bus had been securely locked, the tour guide pointed out the famous spots of Harlem for us, including a building where the body of one of the Kennedy kids had been found with a drug overdose.

For me, this ride through Harlem highlights all the limitations of cultural tourism. There we were, a busful of tourists. Under the supervision of the guide, we gazed at Harlem safely through the glass, with the lens of someone interested in presenting the United States as not only advanced and prosperous but also tolerant of the quaint lifestyles of ethnic enclaves. The glass partition guaranteed that the "culture" of Harlem remained an object separated from and studied by those on the bus. The tour guide's portable voice amplifier made sure that the diverse points of view held by those inside and outside the bus were overpowered by the guide's. So at the end of the tour, we all went our separate ways with bits and pieces of new information neatly tucked away in our minds: a few glimpses of the people and streets of Harlem, a list of names and events associated with it, and, for some of us, a few thoughts on some of the things ignored by the guide. There was no exchange among the people on the bus. Nor did any of us on the bus attempt to find out the views of people living in Harlem, not to mention any possibility of being challenged and reshaped by their views.

Variations of this type of cultural tourism take place around us all the time. For instance, it is not unusual in college classrooms for a professor to assign a text in which an unfamiliar culture is discussed and then to lecture on the main points being made about that culture without analyzing the particular perspective toward that culture taken by the author of the text or the professor himself in his interpretation of it. It is also fairly standard in some classrooms to expect students to do no more than imbibe and regurgitate the points of view of these authorities by taking class notes and doing multiple-choice tests designed to evaluate their ability to retain these views. Other examples of this lack of attention to the perspective shaping the tour can be found, ironically, in instances where special cautions are taken to make certain that the tour is conducted by an "authentic," local guide. For example, a few years ago, a library interested in promoting multiculturalism decided to organize a lecture series on books by "ethnic" writers. Upon finding out that I would be teaching a course titled "Writings from the Borderlands" in which I'd be using many of the books included in the series, the series coordinator asked me if I would lecture on Maxine Hong Kingston's novel *Woman Warrior*. I thought it would be nice if I could give the lecture after I'd had a chance to discuss the book with the students in my class so that I could talk in my lecture about how we negotiated the potential differences in cultural positions taken by the writer, teacher, students, and characters rather than just giving the lecture audience my interpretation of the book. But there was a schedule conflict. The lecture series was scheduled for the first two months of the term, and I would not be using Kingston's book until the end of term. How about having me do the lecture on another book in the series instead, I asked. For instance, I'd just finished teaching Judith Ortiz Cofer's book *Silent Dancing* and would love to talk about how my class and I read it. After a long and awkward silence at the other end of the phone, the coordinator mumbled something about the need to match the book with the speaker. Being Chinese rather than Puerto Rican, it seemed, I didn't "match."

One of the assumptions operating behind this tendency to match the site with the guide, I believe, is cultural tourism's equation of authentic knowledge of a culture with membership in that culture through birth. Following such logic, my authority to guide a tour through a book on Chinese culture is guaranteed by my having been born a Chinese and thus my ability to pass as a local. This assumption identifies perspectives shaping my interpretation of the book as unequivocally at the center of and one with those of all Chinese: Kingston, the characters in her book, or others who live in places like the ones Kingston portrays. This assumption ignores the ways in which particular perspectives, such as my experience of alienation in Chinatowns or my preference for postmodern narrative style, might mediate my view of the book. In fact, for cultural tourism, attention to such factors could be only an unwelcome complication of the authority of the guide and a distraction from the smooth transmission of knowledge that ought to take place during the tour. It is precisely my obvious "Chineseness" that would call attention to the issue of perspective, and that automatically disqualifies me as a guide to a book such as *Silent Dancing*, which would require a Puerto Rican guide.

In opposition to such cultural tourism as an approach to cultural difference, I want to suggest that instead, when viewing and talking about diverse cultures, we represent and negotiate cultural differences in the contact zone. The image of a contact zone, a social space where cultures grapple with one another, can focus our energy on the asymmetrical relations of power existing within and among cultures and on the need to bring about change in these power relations. To go back to my example of the bus tour, approaching Harlem in the contact zone would push me to do four things I didn't do during the tour: 1) view the cultures represented by the people within and outside the bus in terms of their interrelationships and interactions; 2) attend to the differences within these cultures cutting along lines such as race, gender, class, sexual orientation, profession, education, and religion; 3) approach the differences within and among these cultures in the context of their often asymmetrical power relationships; 4) consider ways of renegotiating such relationships following the purpose of multiculturalism. For most of us on the bus, to approach cultural differences in the contact zone would mean setting aside our privileges, forsaking the shelter of the glass partitions, and eliminating the amplification of the tour guide's voice so that we could grapple with the voices of those shut out by such privileges. And as Pratt notes of the contact zone, it would require that we import a lifeway in which "no one is excluded and no one is safe," a lifeway which might reshape each of us in radically different ways (39).

This is no small job for anyone, for it will involve each of us in continuing struggle against our existing habits of thinking about cultural differences and revision of our existing knowledge of ourselves and the world around us. For example, I remember feeling pretty "liberal" during the tour through Harlem: I'd made an effort to know more about an unfamiliar culture, and I had managed to become more knowledgeable about its distinctiveness without condemning it. I could now claim that I was there, had seen this and that, and I knew x, y, and z about Harlem when topics such as the Harlem Renaissance or Black Non-Standard Dialect surfaced. Looking back, I think my liberal complacency came mostly from my then unequivocal sense of my identity: I was a Chinese graduate student of English. This sense of myself allowed me to dissociate from two groups I perceived as implicated in the economic and racial discrimination taking place in Harlem: a white corporate America and a so-called "Chinatown" that I took to consist mostly of small business owners and employees who I believed viewed all blacks as stupid, lazy, violent, and dishonest. I felt I was able to transcend these groups' economic interests and their ignorance of the rich cultural heritage of Harlem.

The concept of a contact zone, with its emphasis on interaction, asymmetrical power relationships, and radical change would challenge such liberal complacency about cultural diversity. When I told myself I was this and not that, I was representing cultural diversity in two ways. In identifying myself as a Chinese, I was depicting cultural differences in terms of a world divided between black, white, and Chinese cultures. In identifying myself as a graduate student, I was projecting a world divided into corporate, academic, and small-business cultures. In each case, I had depicted myself as solidly within one and outside the other two. I was also representing cultural differences politically by acting as a spokesperson for the interests of only one of the three cultures. That is, I was mostly speaking in the interests of the so-called "highly educated" within the Chinese community.

In trying to revise such a form of representation in the contact zone, I would have to put my depiction of cultural difference in the context of the asymmetrical power relations among these cultures in contemporary U.S. society. For instance, my self-representation as a Chinese graduate student of English had privileged the viewpoint of an academic culture, one which believes that its interest in scholarship can enable its members to transcend the material interests and the racist ignorance of the other groups. The ethos of multiculturalism would also require that I try to be accountable for the interests of the least powerful groups in my two representations of the United States: the interests of the African Americans in a society cut by racial divisions and the interests of small business in a society dominated by economic and educational capital. For example, I could consider how employees in a grocery store in Chinatown or Harlem might respond to my liberal condescension. This question could lead me to consider why only "they," not "I," were working for a small business located in a place such as Chinatown or Harlem. This might in turn help me bring back into awareness the ways in which one's access to formal education and fluency in written English affect one's ability to obtain jobs outside small business and in locations other than Chinatown and Harlem. This line of thinking points to the extent to which standard English and educational certification divide the United States and protect the interests of the educated, including people like myself as well as members of white corporate America. As a result, it would make problematic my assumed separation from white corporate America and help me instead to acknowledge my implication in all forms of exclusion perpetuated by the social power of standard English and formal education taking place in Harlem and Chinatown. The only way I might disrupt rather than perpetuate the asymmetrical power relationships would be to search for the viewpoints of members of the so-called uneducated in Harlem and Chinatown and to let these points of view confront and grapple with my "educated" approach to cultural differences. My grasp of the political dimension of my self-representation as a graduate student would also remind me of my interests in speaking as a Chinese American. This ought to push me to attend to the differences in the kind and degree of racial and educational discrimination experienced by members of the African American and Chinese American communities as a result of the slavery of blacks in U.S. history, so that the viewpoints of the least powerful of the three racial groups depicted in my self-positioning—the African American culture and people—could grapple with the views of the other cultures.

In short, the concept of the contact zone would challenge any complacency toward my existing knowledge of myself, Harlem, white corporate America, and Chinatown small business. Instead, it would point to the need to struggle against my existing habits of talking and thinking and to search for alternative and oppositional points of view. And it would map out lines of inquiry to be used for revising my existing knowledge of myself and of cultural differences. Living cultural diversity in a contact zone poses challenges for most of us because it works against powerful beliefs which have become common sense in today's United States. To begin with, life in the contact zone rejects the notion of an authentic self. Instead of affirming the belief that there is some kind of stable essence within each of us called "me"—an essence guaranteed by one's skin color, nationality, ethnic heritage, biological features, and so on—the concept of the contact zone teaches us to perceive one's self as continually being formed and reformed. Furthermore, this self is seen as made and changed through interaction with others in the process of negotiating with those with less—as well as more—privilege than oneself. This image of a self in the making challenges our faith in freedom of self-expression. It asks us to assume accountability for the operation of power in any expression of the self. For the freedom of the privileged is oftentimes grounded in the oppression of an other. Life in the contact zone also pushes us to work against our belief in pluralistic consensus. Instead of assuming that we all have a right to think and act as we choose without consequence, we perceive our personal choices as actions which can have effects on the often unequal distribution of the power across cultures. Thus, it requires that each of us envision ourselves as actively negotiating rather than passively observing cultural differences when approaching "alien" peoples and cultures.

In addition to challenging common beliefs in the unchanging essence of the self and freedom of expression, the concept of the contact zone also challenges the view of knowledge as a commodity. As cultural critics have repeatedly pointed out, dominant institutions in the United States are structured to promote the smooth transaction of goods rather than to enhance confrontation and change. One of these "goods" is knowledge, especially knowledge that has been commodified, backed up by seemingly self-evident facts yielding definitive explanations of things. In this view, the authority of a cultural broker rests on the knowledge she possesses and her ability to pass that knowledge on to others. Life in the contact zone, on the other hand, requires each of us to shift attention away from knowledge transmission toward the process by which knowledge is made: to examine the institutional source of our right to study and know and our access to the means of knowing. Life in the contact zone promotes the act of revision, encouraging each of us to constantly re-view and re-make our existing knowledge by experimenting with points of view oppositional to and suppressed by the views that we each habitually employ. Such a lifeway could produce radical changes in our personal lives and in society, changes which for most of us would involve sharing privileges and power taken for granted as rightly ours. The contact zone makes the transaction of knowledge a risky business. Our authority can no longer be ensured by the amount of knowledge we currently have. Rather, we are constantly pushed to challenge and revise the very knowledge we believe ourselves to have acquired.

Let me use a short story by Sandra Cisneros, "Little Miracles, Kept Promises," to argue for a form of discussion representative of life in the contact zone. "Little Miracles, Kept Promises" has appeared regularly in anthologies on multicultural issues because of the identity of the author and its subject matter. The author has been identified as multicultural because of her Mexican American cultural heritage and because her writing portrays life within the Latino community in Chicago and Texas (Vitale). "Little Miracles," as the editors of one anthology put it, tells a story about a tradition which "consists entirely of letters to saints. In keeping with Mexican tradition, these letters are left before a statue of the saints along with a...little miracle—a small charm" (Colombo, Cullen, and Lisle, 221). The letters are written by characters living in Texas border towns and are about life in those communities. Most of the characters mingle Spanish and English in their speech and writing.

To resist the tendency to tour the culture and people represented in the story as an exotic community separate from the lives of the reader, when discussing the story we need to do more than merely state one another's opinions. Rather, we need to shift our attention from what each of us has to say about the story to the potential asymmetrical relations of power within and between the cultures represented by the reader, the author, and the characters. And we need to discuss one another's opinions by reviewing and revising them in the context of those relations. Let me illustrate by considering responses to one of the twenty-seven letters in Cisneros' story, which reads as follows:

> Dear San Martin de Porres,
>
> Please send us clothes, furniture, shoes, dishes. We need anything that don't eat. Since the fire we have to start all over again and Lalo's disability check ain't much and don't go far. Zulema would like to finish school but I says she can just forget about it now. She's our

> oldest and her place is at home helping us out I told her. Please make her see some sense. She's all we got.
>
> Thanking you,
>
> Adelfa Vasquez
>
> Escobas, Texas

When reading the story, many of my students have tended to see this letter as an example of the gender divisions in what they call "Mexican culture." Here is how one student responded:

> The Mexican culture seems to be inundated with gender roles that members of the American culture would consider archaic and old-fashioned. For instance, there is an important reference to the roles Mexican women are expected to fulfill in Adelfa Vasquez's letter. She is praying to the saints to make Zulema "see some sense" that "her place is at home helping us out." Zulema, the letter reveals, would like to finish her schooling but is needed to do chores at her home. If Zulema were male would she be allowed to pursue an education in order to improve his [sic] life? The reader gets the sense that, yes, were she male, Zulema would be allowed to finish her schooling and the burden of household tasks would fall completely on the shoulders of Adelfa. But since Zulema is a woman, her place is "at home helping [Adelfa] out." Cisneros writes about the attitudes in Mexican culture concerning the role to be played by the females.

Learning to live diversity in the contact zone would mean that we don't stop at responding by a shake or nod of the head or "sharing" our own opinions with the student. Rather, both speaker and listener learn to chart the opposing terms used by the speaker to distinguish and rank different groups, such as the binaries of American vs. Mexican and male vs. female.

For example, attention to the binary of American vs. Mexican and male vs. female might help us examine the ways in which the student depicts Adelfa's cultural position. The third, fifth, and sixth sentences of the student's paper depict Adelfa as a mother interested in having her daughter share "the burden of household tasks." This depiction puts Adelfa at the center of a Mexican culture which expects its female members to stay home and do household chores. The concept of a contact zone, however, would demand that we review this form of depiction in the context of the asymmetrical power relations between Americans and Mexicans in today's world. Since the student depicts Adelfa at the center of the less powerful culture, we have the responsibility to reread Adelfa's letter to search for potential points of view expressed in her letter which might clash and grapple with the viewpoint established by the student. We might notice that in the student's third sentence, the reference to Adelfa's letter deletes Adelfa's description of Zulema as "our oldest." If we were to focus on this part of Adelfa's description, which both Adelfa and Cisneros seem to foreground, we would have to add a question to the one asked in the fourth sentence of the student paper: If Zulema were not the oldest, would Adelfa let Zulema finish school? In the context of Adelfa's letter, the answer could be yes. This line of rethinking would make our initial certainty that Adelfa is unequivocally interested in perpetuating the gender divisions of a culture called "Mexican" somewhat problematic. Our recognition of a need to revise our portrayal of Adelfa's position can then motivate us to look for more aspects of Adelfa's reasoning, undercut by the way she is represented in opinions similar to those voiced in the student paper.

We might notice that an addition has been made to Adelfa's statement. For example, the paper suggests that Adelfa wants Zulema home to help with household chores. Yet, Adelfa's letter indicates no explicit interest in getting more help for household chores. Adelfa seems more interested in another kind of help: getting "things" that can feed and shelter her family. Out of a seven-sentence letter, the first three sentences refer explicitly to such needs. "Home" in Adelfa's letter is not portrayed as burdened by "chores" but by a fire, the need for "anything that don't eat," and a "disability check" which "ain't much and don't go far." This interest in things which feed and shelter is completely ignored in the student paper. The only sentence in the student paper which remotely touches on the issue of economic struggle is the fourth sentence, where improvement of life is presented as the automatic result of schooling. This sentence implies that the economic stress of Adelfa's family is caused by either their lack of education or their old-fashioned attitudes toward education, especially the education of female members of the community. However, if we listen to how other characters in the story discuss their economic distress, it seems that the dire conditions of Adelfa's family can also be related to the kind of job discrimination experienced by members of her community .

So far, we have located three types of interests underlying this student's approach to Adelfa's letter: an interest in contesting the asymmetrical power relationships along gender lines, an interest in presenting education as a means to economic advancement, and a lack of interest in representing the concerns of the economically underprivileged. One way of revising this reading in a contact-zone discussion would be to complicate the approach by acknowledging the divisions generated by economic class. Another related direction for revision is to consider the intersection of class, ethnic, or gender divisions. It seems that our failure to fully represent the interests of the economically and educationally disadvantaged will only get in the way of our interest in breaking down gender divisions.

This revision would not be possible if we did not also tackle another aspect of this student's reading: the tendency to separate and rank the culture some of us call our own against the cultures represented in the story. For example, the second sentence notes that in the letter there is a "reference to the roles Mexican women are expected to fulfill." How would people like Adelfa, Zulema, and Cisneros respond to this portrayal of Adelfa as a "Mexican" woman? Why do some of us feel so comfortable calling someone "Mexican" when she is depicted as living in Texas? In calling the residents of Texas border towns "Mexican," are some of us who identify ourselves as Americans dissolving the implications of our actions in the lifeways portrayed in the story? What difference might it make to identify Adelfa's troubles as those of an "American" rather than a "Mexican"? What might be the reasons for not making such an identification? What can be its consequences? This line of inquiry might help us consider forms of identification employed by residents of the Texas border towns within and outside the story, such as finding out what words writers like Cisneros or Gloria Anzaldua use to describe these border residents in relation to both cultures. To what extent might these alternative names contest and break the lines separating and protecting the privileges of white middle-class American culture from the culture of Mexican Americans?

For example, in posing a Mexican against an American, we run the risk of overlooking the involvement of those calling themselves "Americans" in the economic distress Cisneros depicts Adelfa's family as experiencing. In writing about the Mexican American community as if it were located outside of the American border, we imply that people identified as American have nothing to do with the economic, gender, and educational stress portrayed in the story. Recognizing this should help us to be vigilant and to combat ideological blind spots in our approach to stories like Cisneros': our lack of attention to or interest in economic and class conflict and our tendency to exclude and even expel peoples and cultures different from what we think of as our own.

Learning to live diversity in the contact zone can be unsettling for all of us. As indicated by my rereading of my tour through Harlem and by the discussion I suggest might unfold around one student's opinion of Cisneros' story, life in the contact zone aims at pushing us to yield what we have, including our existing habits of thinking and using language, our existing knowledge of ourselves and others, and the privileges and authority we enjoy and take for granted. It invites us to cause waves, to ask how and why rather than just nodding politely to statements with which we agree or disagree. It also reminds us of the material consequences of our reading and writing. To represent and negotiate cultural differences from the perspective of a less powerful other can disperse and dissolve what had appeared to be solid ground, the foundation of one's life and dreams. It can bring confusion and pain, when every part of our sense of self is engaged or grappled with by voices reminding us of the forms of domination we perpetuate in the choices we make when envisioning who we are and who we aspire to be. Letting go of the glass partition on the tourist bus can bring material consequences—the possibility of becoming a stranger, an "other," to those dear and close to oneself.

However, although a majority of the people I encounter seem initially unwilling to consider their own involvement in all forms of cultural exclusion, they are also eager to identify with democratic ideals such as justice, equality, and freedom for all. Because hegemonic culture seems to have so successfully led most of us to identify these values as classically American, I believe that we can actively mobilize what might be called the moral power of American democratic ideals—the principles of justice, equality, and freedom—to pressure ourselves to overcome our fear of entering a contact zone where diverse cultures and people meet, clash, and grapple with one another. We can use multicultural writings such as Cisneros' story to call attention to the gap between a democratic ideal and the reality of the American society we have in the present and have had in the past. Calling attention to that gap can motivate students to carry out their aspirations for justice, equality, and personal freedom in the very process of reading and writing about cultural differences.

Let me make one last return to my tour metaphor to illustrate the difficulty of the task facing those of us interested in life in the contact zone. The example of my tour in Harlem, I hope, will help to keep in mind both the imaginary and material function of thinking and talking about cultural diversity and thus serve as a cautionary note on what the kind of discussion and reflection I propose can and cannot do. The concept of a contact zone can help us imagine an approach to multicultural issues which seeks out rather than excludes voices and points of view silenced on the touring bus. At the same time, for most of us to physically step outside that bus in the United States of today will involve more than breaking the mental block keeping us sheltered behind the glass, a mental block which the image of the contact zone can help to break. For the United States to become a social space where multiple Americas intersect in the context of equal relations of power will involve social and political rather than conceptual and linguistic changes. At the same time, visions of a different and truly united America are the necessary points of departure for a critical perspective on the here and now of ourselves and our nation. Therefore, in calling your attention to the limited scope of living diversity in our thinking and talking, I also want to remind you of its power to bring about discontent and social change. The kind of cultural work this type of reflection and discussion can do is probably best illustrated by the debate over so-called political correctness orchestrated by a new wave of conservatives in the media. History has taught those of us on the fringe that we must be doing something right if all of a sudden we become a worthy topic, or should I say target, of the conservative media.

Conservative arguments against PC claim that the academy is dominated by a group of radical teachers who impose their version of politically correct positions on diversity and multiculturalism on colleagues and students, thereby suppressing the freedom of speech of those who dare disagree. But for teachers like myself, the core of our conflict with these conservatives is whether or not to call one another's attention to the politics of assigning and assuming particular points of view and not others. Unlike conservatives, we want to call attention to each individual's need and right to deliberate over decisions about where and how to position oneself in relation to diverse cultures. And we need to shift attention from the amount of knowledge we have of diverse cultures to the process by which we have come to adopt and assume a particular form of knowledge and to reflect on the politics of such knowledge-making. For those of us truly interested in a multicultural United States, PC must stand for power and conflict, politics and commitment, rather than for political correctness. The central message we need to get across is that no position, textual or otherwise, can be taken in isolation from the power relationships among diverse cultures with conflicting political interests.

Works Cited

Cisneros, Sandra. "Little Miracles, Kept Promises." Reprinted in Colombo, Cullen, and Lisle, eds., *Rereading America*, 221-32.

Colombo, Gary, Robert Cullen, and Bonnie Lisle, eds. *Rereading America: Cultural Contexts for Critical Thinking and Writing*. 2d ed. Boston: Bedford, 1992.

Pratt, Mary Louise. "Arts of the Contact Zone." *Profession* (1991): 33-40.

Vitale, Tom. "Interviews with Writers." Tape interview of Sandra Cisneros by Tom Vitale. In *A Moveable Feast* , #9250.

Chapter 7

The Accidental Culture: Disability and the Enduring Need for Closure

James A. Helten

It is human folly not so much to attempt to achieve closure where there is none but, rather, to expect to and to allow our inability to do so to paralyze us and to damn us to a life of inaction and silence. Closure itself takes many forms, including that of a final, immutable truth about a topic which should mark a conclusion to the discussion or presentation. When applied to human lives, a sense of closure may be achieved by identifying a defining characteristic or feeling a certainty about how our lives may end or proceed from a given point. Yet, closure is not so much a belief in destiny or fate as it is a faith in a birthright. The more democratic a society becomes the less certain it is that individual members (or groups) are blessed or cursed by birthright, regardless of the economic or social strata into which we are born. But it is human nature, nonetheless, to continue to search for a birthright to provide our lives direction and impetus in this increasingly chaotic world.

Frank Kermode, professor of literature and noted literary theorist, in his book *The Sense of an Ending*, examines and compares the ways humankind, throughout its history, has attempted to make sense of the lives of human beings. "Men, like poets, rush into the middest when they are born [where they also die], and to make sense of their span they need fictive concords with origins and ends, such as give meaning to lives and poems.... We project ourselves—a small, humble elect, perhaps—past the End, so as to see the structural whole, a thing we cannot do from our spot of time in the middle" (7-8). Humans, he maintains, cannot tolerate brute, inchoate, discrete realities, and so we may find in the records of our existence historical, theological, philosophical, scientific, and literary fictions that attempt to reconcile "the middest" with our origins and our ends. (The Bible provides our most striking paradigm with its Genesis and Apocalypse bounding the earthly history of humankind.)

The human race, Kermode says, for millennia essentially was satisfied with a version of its origin finally settled on, but constantly altered its projection of an end as additional knowledge was acquired. Hence, the fictions kept changing. (He is dealing only with the Judeo-Christian tradition of rectilinear time.) Within the past several centuries of scientific discoveries regarding the biological basis of life, the long-held concept of our origin also was challenged, reinterpreted, and subsequently in need of new fictions. In this current century, especially, our end has become no longer naively imminent (about to happen), he says, but rather has become immanent, a shadow which lies on the crises of our fictions (inherent in them). If Kermode is correct, as I suspect he is, then my own obsession with achieving closure in writing about disabilities appears to be a universal basic human need that serves to illuminate a critical and defining aspect of my own life—the psychological transformation that occurred in me as a direct result of becoming physically disabled at an age when my identity as an able-bodied young adult had already developed sufficiently to become firmly entrenched in my psyche. (For example, in my dreams I am still most frequently able-bodied, although my walking may be labored or I may feel pleased that it is not.) Thus it is that twenty-seven years after suffering a permanent, disabling injury, I find it so difficult to write about either my individual experience or my cultural one. I know that I cannot achieve closure on the topic, either as a projection of what the future holds or as an immutable truth about it that defines the experience for me or for others. It is the tension created by my desire for closure and my distrust of any that I find that enables me to draw from my experience of being disabled to guide me in my professional life. It helps to know how you function, not because you realistically can desist from that behavior completely, or even modify it substantially so that it no longer seems to be the obstacle that it once was, but because knowledge of the behavior might enable you to become more self-tolerant, appreciating your motivation and, perhaps, even finding an advantage in it. My point in this seeming self-indulgence is that I have learned something important about closure that has had a significant and lasting impact on the way I attempt to teach my students the art of writing. As often happens, that knowledge has carried over into my thinking about disabilities and multiculturalism and aided me in finding meaning and coherence in those apparently disparate topics as they intersect.

As an assistant professor in the department of English of a small historically black college in North Carolina, I teach courses in freshman composition that emphasize effective uses of argumentation in writing. For the past several years, I have structured the course work around a theme of multiculturalism: the rights and the responsibilities of the majority and the rights and responsibilities of the minority in a diverse multicultural democratic society (majority and minority often not as numerical absolutes but as designations in relation to the status quo). One of my goals is for my students to begin to recognize the existence of diverse cultures and *types* of cultures in our society, the multicultural nature of individuals, the capacity for most individuals to slip readily from one culture into another at will, and the frequency with which we do it. Students become more capable of recognizing the interchangeable roles of majority and minority in the diverse cultures that they experience when they acquire a basis for appreciating the obvious benefits of being of the majority or minority in different contexts.

Many students come to class initially with an immature and narrow notion of the rhetorical implications of argument. To many, successful argument in class discussions includes shouting down anyone with a point of view differing from their own, employing intimidating body language to support their point of view, disregarding generally accepted rules of evidence, and proudly proclaiming closure on classic and current controversial issues that wouldn't remain controversial if resolution were so easily attainable. As they perceive the task, arguments exist only to be won or lost.

I try to tease my students into thought by suggesting that a dominating speaker in an argument is more often the true loser than is the listener. The speaker only hears what he or she already knows and, therefore, gains little of lasting value in the exercise (a loser in the long run). The listener has the opportunity to learn about opposing points of view and supporting evidence and to adjust his or her point of view to coincide with current evidence and consequently is a winner, regardless of immediate and temporary resolution of the issue. My insistence that learning should be the true aim of argument generally is not appreciated. In place of closure as the only fitting resolution in argumentation, I suggest to them the idea of "dissensus," a concept I was led to investigate initially as some form of resolution to the conflicts with the world I personally came to encounter as a result of becoming permanently physically disabled at the same age as these freshman students—when my view of myself no longer coincided with the view of me held by the world. Dissensus aided me also when I had internalized the conflict—when the view I had of my able-bodied self no longer coincided with the view of my disabled self.

Dissensus, the agreeing to disagree as a temporary resolution to a conflict, has little appeal for my students, since it appears to entail neither final and absolute resolution (a form of closure) nor approbation of their a priori positions (also a form of closure). Its main use is as a refuge for the presumed loser of a debate who is not amenable to modifying his or her stand in the face of overwhelming evidence suggesting the need to do so. Dissensus is righteously proclaimed by students in self-defense through the use of phrases such as "Well, I have a right to my own opinion, no matter what you say!" and "In conclusion, everybody needs to make his own decision about this issue!" As I struggle to find more effective means of demonstrating the broader values and aims of argumentation and of dissensus, I am forced to reexamine the relevance the notion has for disabled persons experiencing cultural conflict with society and personal psychological conflict as a result of an enduring physical trauma that, against their wills, has come to define them.

The Culture of Disability: A Brief History

To my knowledge, no general history focusing on the lives of disabled persons has been published, nor have I been able to identify any major research project of the subject, although such an academically attractive endeavor should prove to be of wide interest and value in this age of cultural studies and multiculturalism. What I present here is no more than a sketchy, impressionistic interpretation and rendering of ideas and information I have encountered during many years of academic studies and civil rights advocacy for various disability groups.

The "culture of disability" is widely considered to comprise at least four dramatically disparate subcultures: visually-impaired persons, hearing-impaired persons, mentally-impaired persons, and mobility-impaired persons (the latter currently the largest and least homogeneous of the groups). When conveniently thrown together as they often are for social, educational, and recreational purposes, individuals of the subcultures traditionally respond in a negative manner, resenting and resisting the lumping together and stereotyping, circling their cultural wagons in four distant corners to reassert the separate identity of each.

Physically, the members of the subcultures have very little in common, although their experiences of isolation from and an assumed inferiority to general society gives them more in common than they are willing to recognize. Unfortunately, the subcultures have a history of mutual antipathy, stemming from divergent needs for accommodation from society in order to function daily on as near a basis of equality as possible. The resources available for making physical accommodations are limited, and the competition for them is great. In addition, the subcultures appear hesitant to compound the reasons for their cultural status by assuming the stigma that comes with being identified with more diverse and possibly less socially attractive persons than themselves. That single dynamic has served to nullify attempts at political cooperation between the groups in the United States for many decades. Nonetheless, the four subcultures were able to unite as a culture of the whole in recent times to promote passage of the Rehabilitation Act of 1972 and the Americans with Disabilities Act of 1990.

In the process of cooperating to achieve passage of legislation, groups and individuals who did not want to be further stigmatized by publicly aligning themselves with persons of other disabilities found themselves facing their own prejudices and learning to deal with them in a productive manner. As a bonus, confronted by needs for architectural accessibility to society, the various groups discovered underlying currents of mutual interest and benefit that provide a basis for future cooperation. People in wheelchairs require beveled curbs, elevators, and larger restroom stalls, for example. If the beveled curbs are not created with a surface texture signaling to blind persons that the construction is in place, the loss of the normal curb can unwittingly lead a person using a white cane directly into the flow of automobile traffic. Programmatically, Equal Opportunity legislation for employment and education can be administered more efficiently for all groups through a single system. Further examples of mutual benefits abound and become more apparent with each combined effort.

Interests shared with the general public were emphasized when women with baby buggies, aging persons, and other walkers were found often to prefer to use beveled curbs and ramps where they exist alongside regular curbs and stairs. Historically, benefits shared by the disabled and nondisabled have been great, although they have been largely unheralded. For example, the early inventors of the typewriter were searching for a means to make written communications easier for blind people.

The Dregs of Society

I remember reading in Ann Landers's column or in Dear Abby about ten years ago a letter from a woman complaining that our nation's wars always cost the lives of so many of our healthy, morally upright young men. She asked why the nation couldn't improve society as a whole by sending to die, instead, the drug addicts, criminals, and disabled persons who bring ruin upon our society. As I remember it, the response was that neither our nation nor any nation could afford to entrust its safety to the "dregs of society." Lumping disabled people with the drug addicts and criminals of our society does an unconscionable disservice to persons who, as a group, are already fighting an overwhelming stigma. To identify them further as the "dregs of society" does additional damage. That view of disabled persons, however, is one that is still widely held and difficult to change.

Individuals with physical and mental disabilities have existed within human societies since the earliest of recorded time, as historical and literary documents attest, and as reports from archeological digs of ancient sites around the world confirm. As victims of wars, farming and hunting accidents, pestilences, and the vagaries of genetics, disabled persons have played diverse roles in society. A few fortunate blind persons in antiquity enjoyed the status of educators and bards (the Greek epic poet Homer, for instance), and of "seers" interpreting the oracles of the gods, such as the fictional Tiresias in Homer's *Iliad*. But many more of them, their stories largely untold, were assigned menial tasks such as basket weaving, or had to beg for a living, becoming burdens to their families and their tribes. While deaf persons could handle the roles of professional craftsmen such as marble workers and blacksmiths and engage in farming and hunting, they were often thought to be mentally incompetent. In superstitious cultures people who were mentally impaired often were believed to be touched by the hands of the gods and were boons to the tribe. Many Native American cultures believed that individuals like the "contrary" of Lakota Sioux culture were favorites of the Great Spirit and were protected by neighboring tribes as well as their own. In other cases they were treated as punishments from the gods visited upon a disobedient people. Most often, they were treated as perpetual children with the capacity for only the most menial of labor. Many cultures abandoned physically deformed and other unwanted children in the wilderness (as some still do). Those persons surviving abandonment were likely to eventually succumb to unenlightened medical procedures such as "bleeding" to rid the body of malevolent "humors" that were believed to be the cause of congenital and traumatic disabilities.

Mobility-impaired persons (those who suffered the loss or function of at least one limb) sometimes fared better as contributing and integral members of a culture than other disabled persons. Injured in battle or in a hunting accident, they might be otherwise hale and hearty fellows, retaining old roles or finding alternative life-sustaining roles as craftsmen in their villages. A hunter or warrior who lost a leg to amputation might pick up another trade that did not require as much mobility or travel, but relied more on the use of two healthy arms, as a producer of weapons, for instance. This lot shouldn't be misconstrued as having better fortune in general, for large numbers of them died at the time of injury from loss of blood or shortly thereafter from complications such as gangrene. Persons who suffered injuries to their spinal cords generally died within brief periods after their accidents, victims of urinary tract infections for which there were no antibiotics.

Perhaps, many more physically disabled people suffered a life similar to that of Aesop, the ancient Greek collector of tales, whose body was tragically malformed from birth. His face was so disfigured that he was blind in one eye and nearly so in the other, and his limbs were twisted so that he was practically immobile. With his wife and his children, he lived in near isolation from people, presumably because of the mistreatment he received.

Social, political, and economic conditions for disabled persons did not begin to improve until modern times. In the 1800s, schools for blind and deaf people were created to train them in useful occupations, often as the result of the work of philanthropic individuals and groups. Blind persons who socialized with other blind persons, often for the first time, could communicate more independently over long distances using braille, and could be trained for the new, stereotypical occupation of piano tuning, for, as everyone seemed to know, blind persons customarily developed a compensatory sense of hearing that particularly suited them to such a vocation; musicianship proved possible only for the truly gifted. They were valued by society because of their stereotypical constant cheerfulness and their capacity to make sighted people around them feel blessed in comparison, a legacy still operating today. For persons with hearing impairments the story was radically different, due largely to communication difficulties between the deaf individual and society (a difficulty overcome, though, within families and with close friends). Deaf persons communicate effectively with each other using sign language, but not with society, which has made no concerted effort to learn that language. Communicating with pad and pencil, though laborious, requires no significant effort to learn or adapt on the part of nondeaf persons. As a consequence of the communication problem, hearing-impaired persons developed a culture unto themselves earlier than other groups, interacting with the speaking and hearing world only when they went to work, often as print shop and newspaper employees, where the din of the printing presses they operated already drowned out audiocommunication between workmen and threatened to deafen hearing employees. Bakeries also became frequent employers of deaf persons, perhaps because they were believed to have developed a compensatory sense of smell useful in the business.

Mentally-impaired persons fared least well in the process of being integrated into society. They were isolated in individual homes or herded into dingy, overpopulated asylums where they were taught no common trade, learned few socialization skills, and were abandoned by society to languish in every manner. They were with "others of their kind," society rationalized, happy to become, in some perverse manner, their own "dis-culture." In the last two decades, the doors of many asylums and state institutions have been thrown open, in many cases forcing patients out into a world that is barely more suited to integrate them than was medieval society.

The relatively new subculture of the mobility-impaired comprises the largest subculture of disabled persons (according to government census figures for the last several decades) and is the most rapidly growing one. These individuals require the most substantive and costly accommodations by society to gain even minimal physical access. Initially, the government sought to serve them by institutionalizing them for education or training and for long-term medical treatment, hiding from society both the enormity and the complexity of the task ahead for the nation of becoming architecturally accessible and professionally equitable.

Few Crippled Children's Schools (as they were called until recently) and rehabilitation hospitals existed in this country before the middle of this century, leaving many states not covered by any basic services. The first training programs for paraplegics (paralyzed legs, confined to a wheelchair) focused on making watch repairers of them, since sitting at a workstation all of the workday was a prerequisite for the job and an obvious capability common to the trainees. Ahead for mobility-impaired persons was the most dramatic revolution in the history of the culture of disability, resulting from the dynamic confluence of medical and political forces.

World War II, along with producing the largest population to that time of newly disabled soldiers and civilians, provided a testing ground for sulfa drugs to combat urinary tract infections, the cause of more deaths among people initially surviving spinal cord injuries than all other causes combined. The sheer volume of disabled veterans that overflowed both military and civilian hospitals necessitated the construction of scores of rehabilitation centers specializing in primary medical care, longer-range physical development, psychological adjustment, and vocational planning. The age of rehabilitation medicine had dawned. Before the war ended, at a military rehabilitation hospital in Stoke-Mandeville, England, spinal cord-injured soldiers in wheelchairs, looking for a means of exercise and socialization, took a basketball onto a court for an informal game. From that initial sporting event emerged a sporting empire covering the globe. Persons from nearly all disability types engage in all existing sports for able-bodied athletes that can be modified to accommodate disabilities. Several new sports not envisioned by the able-bodied world have been created where the mere adaptation of existing sports did not meet the needs.

The fifty-year history of the commingling of people with diverse disabilities for social and political purposes, for athletic competition, recreation, and artistic endeavors, and for employment and other activities of mainstream society has resulted in the emergence of a "culture of disability" that seeks and deserves recognition and acceptance as a viable, contributing member of the new multicultural order.

The "Dis" in Disability

Unfortunately, at the core of the conflicts that disabled persons experience with society, with persons of other disabilities, and even with themselves is a negative element the ramifications of which may be lessened frequently, but never totally eliminated. For cultures with social, political, and economic aspirations, language rightly is perceived as power, and control over referential terms for the culture acts as an early test and expression of the power held by the group. There is a general lack of consensus about how persons with various impairments should be referred to collectively, the same dynamic that has engendered much social debate and dissension over appropriate terms to use when referring to African Americans, Hispanics, women, and other culture groups over the course of the last thirty years. In the case of a paraplegic using a wheelchair for mobility, for instance, the terminology previously included "gimp" and "cripple," terms now deemed to be derogatory, especially when used by persons outside the culture (akin to "nigger"). Those terms were replaced by ones carrying less emotional charge and retaining satisfactory degrees of explanatory power—"disabled" and "handicapped." Currently, however, there are political moves afoot to exchange those terms for ones meant to improve once again societywide perceptions of disabled persons—"physically challenged" and "handi-capable." The term "disabled" is employed throughout this essay because it is brief, sufficiently descriptive and differentiating, and unambiguous. The critical point of contention among individuals favoring various terms is not so easily dismissed, though.

In the fall of 1980, when I was just beginning my doctoral work, I took part in a seminar for teaching assistants shortly before the semester began. The director of the Freshman Composition Program and other faculty members contributing to the training were making a special effort to make me feel comfortable in the English department. On our first lunch break I accompanied the director of the program to the department office to check our mailboxes. With the utmost sincerity, he asked me directly, "By the way, what do you prefer to be called? 'Handicapped' or 'disabled'?" I responded in a fashion I hoped would be considered witty and nonchalant: "'Fucked-up' works well for me!" I waited for a laugh. There was none! I was embarrassed at the complete silence my response fostered. I had offended or made uncomfortable the very person who was making a magnanimous attempt to make me feel comfortable and welcome in this new environment. Language is powerful, but also tricky. It's probably best not to fool with terminology in the presence of strangers.

The term "disability" is the most linguistically precise for referring to the population being discussed. The root of the word focuses our attention on the concept of ability, the physical capacity to perform the functions of everyday living in the ergonomic manner for which the human body was designed. Persons with physical disabilities retain many, if not most, of their physical abilities, and with varying degrees of modification they remain capable of performing the tasks of daily living for which they are no longer naturally suited. The qualifier "dis," however, represents not merely the quality of physical or mental unsuitedness for a task, as in inability. It denotes a more pervasive physical inferiority, since the inability in question is one that should not exist in a normal, healthy individual. Additionally, it suggests the power of the language to mold the perceptions of the users of the term, the dynamic which ultimately makes it possible, even probable, that no single term can survive over time the rigors of a test for political correctness, especially when the social status of the subjects being referred to has entered into a state of social flux. De-emphasize political correctness for its changing sensibilities and superficiality and "disability" becomes a dynamic term, as the language of the streets is beginning to suggest.

A transitive verb from the language of the streets is being adopted currently for mainstream use: "to dis," meaning to disrespect—as in, "Hey, man! Are you dissing me?" The "dis" of "disability" has become a word in itself. The word has already made its way from the streets to teens to the Oprah Winfrey show. The word will likely fall out of favor by the time the majority of people learn it, or because they learn it. Nonetheless, dis is a valuable word. Disabilities are not now and will never be mere inabilities, regardless of the terms used to identify them. Changing the term will not bring respect to disabled people who deserve it. Only changing behaviors and the level of awareness society has of disabled people and their accomplishments can do that, or should.

Disability implies many things beyond mere impairment of motor skills. Unjustly or not, it implies unemployability, lack of intelligence, a lower social station, physical pain, failed marriages, substance abuse—the list could be very long, indeed. Many of the negative stereotypes have some basis in fact. Employability for disabled persons is a greater problem than it is for the general population. Self-conscious, alienated disabled persons often manifest difficulties with certain social skills. Chronic, intractable pain is, for some, a fact of daily existence. Marriages taking place before one partner becomes disabled have greater difficulties to surmount, since one of the partners has assumed a new physical and psychological identity which was not a party to the original agreement. Substance abuse is more difficult to avoid for a population with steady access to and legitimate need for prescription drugs which are often more mind-altering than an illegal and socially unaccepted drug such as marijuana. None of these situations may be a part of the life of a particular disabled person, since a disability is a radically different experience for each person. Making assumptions about a group invariably does disservice to many members of that group. Disability also implies fortitude, patience, dedication, and a long list of stereotyped positive characteristics that have some basis in fact, also, but that are individual traits, not features inherited with the disability.

As elusive and vague as it is, the concept of dis resides both in the stereotyping and stigmatizing of an individual which serve to exclude or alienate him or her from the non-dis society. The practical meaning of dis lies in the actual physical impact of the disability on the individual and in the fact that, regardless of the great effort on the part of many individuals to convince themselves otherwise, a disability is not and will never be desirable or attractive, is inherently disadvantageous, is unnatural, and is not purposeful in itself. The meaning of dis provides no possibility for resolution to the conflict that continues to prey on the minds of disabled persons and their support community. If anywhere, the conflict raised by being disabled in a nondisabled society must be addressed personally by affected individuals. Unity within a culture is bolstered by the pride that members take in a readily identifiable common feature. There is no pride to be found in being born disabled or becoming disabled as a result of an accident. The common feature is dis. Realistically, while "Black is beautiful!", disabilities are, at the very least, "unattractive" and "burdensome."

Given the influence society can exert on an individual, nonetheless, it can never disable the individual in the manner or to the degree that an individual can destructively disable him- or herself. Consider the fact that a paraplegic as a mower of lawns is disabled legitimately by his physical condition, as a vacuumer of carpets is disabled to the extent that his attitude encourages him to be (to get out of distasteful and moderately difficult chores), and as a washer of dishes is not truly disabled at all. For the individual, the reality of the disability lies in a dynamic derived from the connection between the person and his or her task, influenced by social expectations and personal attitudes—hence the tendency within this essay to refer to persons as having disabilities and as disabled persons, rather than to "the disabled." Each individual is a person first and foremost, with a very personal and unique relationship with his or her own disability that defines that person much more precisely and accurately than collective terminology can. My choice of terms is only a bit more cumbersome than the shortened form, but it serves as an essential reminder about the enduring personhood of the subject. In addition, each is a member of numerous other cultures that may be slipped into and out of as the situation warrants, cultures that serve more appropriately to define the individual within varying contexts than the context-specific notion of disability.

The Disabled "I"

Everybody has a story. In working and playing and living with persons with disabilities in various capacities over the past twenty-seven years, I'm not sure if I've ever heard the same story twice, although newspaper "human-interest" stories that appear several times a month focus on such superficial details that you begin to feel that if you've read one story you've read them all. That may be as much a necessity of the situation as a fault of the press. It commonly takes a person many years from the onset of a traumatic physical injury to begin to perceive with any degree of sophistication the larger ramifications of what has occurred.

In the early morning of Memorial Day, 1967, ten days before my eighteenth birthday, I was involved in a motorcycle accident, sustaining a traumatic physical injury that significantly altered the course of my life. In addition to breaking most of my teeth and ribs and my right wrist, I fractured the fourth and fifth thoracic vertebrae in my back, bruising and pinching my spinal cord, and permanently paralyzing my legs and lower torso. Prior to that incident, I had found great comfort in my assumption that life had in store for me a successful and happy future prefigured by the family I had been born into and by the academic, athletic, and social stature to which I had risen during my high school years. As a recent graduate with a merit scholarship in mathematics to a state university, I took great pride and pleasure in defining myself also as a football player who, after scoring two touchdowns and a point-after in a single game, lifted his girlfriend by her waist into the air high above him and twirled in delirious circles around and around, confident that he at last had the world in his control. I was a white Catholic male raised in a lower middle-class family in a small town in the upper Midwest. I had absolute faith that I would become a college-educated professional, the husband of a beautiful and intelligent woman, and the father of two and one-third children (who could anticipate lives of greater ease and happiness than their parents had in the same measure that my life would be more fortunate than those of my parents). Life had closure. Life made sense. Life was good.

Several hours after that accident, lying in an intensive care unit of a hospital, I sensed that I had left home for good, although I tried to reassure my crying mother otherwise. I had no notion that my future had changed drastically, only that it might be postponed. My awareness of a need for a new life fiction to take into account this new physical reality dawned as slowly as did my understanding of the true extent of my injuries and of their long-range and permanent ramifications. The need for a new metaphysical relationship with the world also became apparent only gradually as I attempted to reintegrate myself with society once primary physical rehabilitation was completed. Several years after the accident I could see that life had indeed changed, that the incident was having a psychological impact on the manner in which I viewed my life. Gone was the naive sense of an imminent future (to use Kermode's paradigm) and the feelings of comfort and security that attend it; in its stead was a growing recognition that my future, my End, was prefigured in the main by the character of my responses to the crises that had already beset me and would continue to. The evolution of personal conflict due to my disability proceeded in this manner: when graduating from high school I held a view of myself that was generally consonant with the view the world held of me. Initially, when I sustained a permanent physical disability, my self-concept remained essentially the same. In the first few years after I left the sanctuary of the rehabilitation hospital, I gradually became aware that the world's view of me had changed radically for the worse for what I saw as unjust and spurious reasons. However, since the unique opportunity presented itself, I set about attempting to change those psychological aspects of myself that previously had held me back. It would be wonderful, I thought, if I could be less intimidated by the world around me—more socially dynamic and less affected by the opinions of me held by those around me—for instance. With each small victory, I became more convinced that the life I lived before my accident had closed, that I had begun a new and separate life starting again from age one. There was no metaphysical conduit connecting the two lives, except for the memories I retained. I also saw no connection between the me that I created and the me that the world perceived, enabling me to counter the exclusion the world forced onto me with a self-imposed alienation from its hostility. Most dangerously, though, I perceived of my physical and psychological selves as separate entities: my psychological self challenged this new physical self for domination, for the preeminent right to existence. I was searching for new means of achieving closure in my life.

Upon discharge from the rehabilitation hospital, I walked away from the life I had led previously, eschewing nearly all relationships I had built in almost eighteen years, except for most of those with family. I never went to visit the parents of my friend who had died in the same motorcycle accident. Reunions with former friends and classmates seemed pointless. The situation was even more extreme with my father. During high school, my relationship with him had been marked by a tension not uncommon between fathers and sons. After the accident it became openly hostile, so much so that, while I was visiting home for Sunday dinners in May of one year, he kicked me out of the house three times in the space of four weeks. Among other things, our hostility was fueled by the disregard I felt for him that seemed not to be moderated by any familial love. I forgot all that he had done for me over the years and questioned whether or not he actually was my father. I felt absolutely no connection, and I desired none. I needed no father in my new life. (No doubt this break would have occurred even if the accident hadn't. The disability provided the conditions for it to occur earlier and more profoundly, prolonging for my father his role as a caretaker beyond my graduation from high school and postponing my physical independence.)

As an undergraduate college student, I ate in a dining hall that served fifteen hundred students, but that sat no more than seven or eight hundred at a time, which meant eating in shifts and cramming for sitting space at tables. Oftentimes, the only room available would be at a table occupied by the type of young women I might have been dating had I not sustained a disability. Several times when I came to use one free corner of a table otherwise occupied by them, they got up, took their trays, and searched for other seating. The signal they sent hurt so deeply that for a while I initially took my tray, went to eat, and bussed my garbage without looking up from the floor except to avoid collisions. When the hurt turned to anger, I began to search for such situations and stayed an extra long time, eyeing the girls to see how uncomfortable I was making them. But, I never approached them personally or attempted to break the ice. I wanted only to punish them. I was in self-imposed alienation.

In the first twenty years following my injury, I did not once awaken to recall a dream in which I used a wheelchair or was seriously physically impaired. I walked, ran, and jumped as I had as a teenager. In fact, I had dreams in which fellow wheelchair athletes that I had never known as able-bodied persons were walking as I was. My subconscious refused to assimilate the disability. The contradiction in holding on to a self-image I inherited from a life that I felt no longer existed was never apparent to me. I had no desire to end that former life or to deny the former me. I had merely responded to what I believed to be the inexorable need to do so.

As the mythologies and illusions we create for ourselves begin to fade and fail, there comes room for epiphanies that may be ever so delightful and reassuring. Early in my marriage (about ten years after my injury), with the help of a friend I was building a ramp into the "fix-up" house that my wife and I had purchased. On an uncommonly hot day for the area, I was working shirtless and the sweat was rolling down my face and upper torso. From somewhere deep inside me came the sudden and overwhelming impression that "I smell my father in me," the man who had come home from twelve-hour days in his radiator shop with little left about him for his six children but a comforting, identifying smell of hard-earned sweat. It was the first time in my new life that I felt sure that I was my father's son, and it signaled my first steps on a long and arduous journey back to my father, which hasn't yet been completed. I learned just this summer, at the age of forty-five, that my father was among the first American troops to enter Dachau, one of the worst of the Nazi concentration camps for Jews, shortly after it had been liberated at the end of World War II. His task as a bulldozer driver was to bury the smelling, decomposing corpses and clean up the camp. I was stunned to hear of this wartime experience that must serve to define my father in some very significant way, a story that was not even hinted at while I was growing up. I am learning that I do not know my father nearly as well as I thought I did. The process of reintegrating my two selves, recognizing and welcoming the child still in me, was aided immensely by the single impression of smelling my father in me. To finally connect my father with my new self, I first had to connect my old self with my new self. Working and playing with disabled people for many years, I had discovered what I still believe to be an immutable truth about people sustaining a traumatic, permanent injury, a notion which is about as close as I ever may get to achieving any degree of closure—a traumatic injury does not change the basic nature of the individual; instead, it brings it to the fore. If a person was a fighter before the trauma, he or she will be a fighter after it, if a quitter before, then a quitter after, and so on. To see that connection in myself, I first had to conceive that there could be one. From that point on, each step followed the preceding one as needfully, yet as naturally and as inexplicably, as with an infant learning to walk.

The epiphanies continued. As a multisport wheelchair athlete, I regularly played exhibition basketball games against able-bodied men and women using wheelchairs who were completely talentless playing on my turf. Seldom have I been offered camaraderie and respect more quickly and sincerely than from opponents in those games. In distance running (from six kilometers to half-marathons), I have received encouragement from numerous runners on foot as I passed them on the way to the finish line. It is difficult to remain alienated from the openhearted and open-minded fellow competitors I have been blessed to meet.

Ironically, through hard work and good fortune I now have much of the life that I once assumed I would. Although I have no children, I do have a college education, a career that I enjoy, a beautiful, intelligent, and loving wife, and a house that is sufficiently upscale from that of my father. I realize, though, that the life I am leading is not closure for itself. No matter how much I distrust a sense of closure, I still desire it and search for it in many things I do. Since my fiction has changed, I seek a new sense of an Ending to help me find meaning in life here in the middest, that would give me direction and impetus in an otherwise chaotic world. That search, striving and not yielding, is the legacy of the character building of my early years. The conditions in which I must now conduct the search, wary of closure and beset by crises that are in addition to those that most men my age must face, is the legacy of my disability. As disabled people must discover, and as people of all cultures must discover, closure in life is never achieved, yet we must continue to seek it. If we are to judge ourselves, we should do it on the character of our responses to the crises we face that define our humanity.

Work Cited

Kermode, Frank. *The Sense of an Ending, Studies in the Theory of Fiction.* New York: Oxford University Press, 1961.

Chapter 8

No Sentimental Education: An Essay on Transatlantic Cultural Identity

Thomas Austenfeld

You've got to be carefully taught.
—Rodgers and Hammerstein, *South Pacific*

Bibliography may advance politics through semantics. The Library of Congress Subject Guide does not list the adjective "multicultural" as a classification term. Instead, the officially sanctioned term is "intercultural," a coinage that suggests the realm of ideas rather than the arenas of daily life. Cultures, then, interact on both levels: As the "raw" meeting in the marketplace is transformed into a conceptual encounter, a multicultural experience turns into an intercultural reflection. The fortuitous etymological situation in library classification signals a larger truth: cultural competence is played out both in practice and in theory. A culturally cognizant person is always already a participant who is situated at the intersections of cultural exchange. At the same time, this person cares about the theoretical dimensions of culture. Cultural identity thus results from the personal involvement of each human being in his or her context followed by reflection. Such reflection can help to clarify motives, provide historical lines of thought, and give direction to future multicultural encounters.

Drawing on personal experience, I will argue in this essay that a well-defined and reflected self-identity is essential for reasonable and productive discourse to occur in society. With reference to a few high-profile current events, I will attempt to outline the path on which, in my view, the present cultural debate proceeds in the United States. Building on that ground, I will reflect on a seminal incident in my own life that has caused me to rethink the effectiveness of my intercultural education. Finally, I will suggest some educational imperatives.

Participation in a democratic society is a delicate matter and requires a reflected self-identity. Yet in this time of rapid transformations, when a formerly rigid world is in post-Cold War flux and communication is instantaneous, self-identity also needs to be open to change and adaptation. It is apparent that global problems—hunger, pollution, natural resources, sustainability of the planet—which until recently each generation seemed to pass down to the next at minimal risk to itself, now face us directly. Where political power and military prowess used to combine comfortably to maintain the status quo, the imminent overpopulation of our planet forces rich and poor nations alike to reconsider their roles in the world. Consequences for the individual human being result from this reassessment. However circumscribed and parochial one's original identity may be, anybody may be plunged into the midst of a controversy in which ethnic, religious, gender, and other social determinants come together to form a space for debate and exchange of ideas. In the process of adapting from life in Westphalia, the German province of my birth, to life in the United States, I have seen parochial constriction on both sides of the Atlantic. Yet frequently, more than just debate and ideas are at stake. Academics and journalists have the luxury of debating ideas, but even a casual glance at the evening news would suggest that ethnic and religious identity can be a matter of life and death for peoples around the globe.

Intellectual debate in the United States tends to be controversial mostly because relatively little is at stake: academic debates are frequently "academic" in the pejorative sense of the word. Moreover, while scientific discoveries receive immediate public attention—promising outlooks in the research on AIDS come to mind—debates in the humanities tend to have far less of a popular echo, unless a wholesale revolution of hitherto accepted norms and values seems to threaten the peace. A notable exception to the customary wallflower existence of humanities debates has been the heat generated by the controversy over Political Correctness in the past few years. It extended into the popular media and to the Sunday political talk shows until it gradually lost its sting by its codification in legal controversy.

In the United States, cultural debate shares with other public phenomena its eventual relegation to the legal realm. The American impulse to reduce debates to a battle of conflicting rights—to purify them, as it were, in the crucible of law—is difficult for a foreigner to understand. It is premised on the Constitution and its amendments as the founding documents of the country's identity. These written documents take the place in American culture of the national identity in European countries that is based on cultural practice and is shared with preceding generations over hundreds of years. Legal thinking in the United States creates clear fronts. In the abortion debate, for example, the right of the fetus is weighed against the right of the mother. In the PC debate the right to free speech is pitted against the protection from hateful pronouncements. But the intended clarity of opposing viewpoints can have unintended effects.

Much has changed since the relatively amicable discussion over E. D. Hirsch and Allan Bloom and the possibility of a commonly shared American cultural identity. By contrast, at the time of this writing, the great public debate over the incendiary and anti-Semitic remarks made by Khallid Abdul Mohammad at Keane College in November of 1993 has been carried out, not under the terms of Political Correctness, but under the terms mostly of First Amendment rights. While free speech is essential to the American understanding of freedom, historical experience elsewhere may dictate different solutions. Germany, for example, has relatively strict laws against hate speech and the proliferation of anti-Semitic writings. As a result, German neo-Nazis print their pamphlets abroad. Legal codification of the right to controversy raises the tempting popular assumption that whatever I may legally do, I may presume to be ethical. Few fallacies could be more misleading. Legal sanction does not remove personal responsibility.

As a German living in the United States, I have experienced the personal properties of cultural identity more strongly than my education ever led me to expect. Outside of the fatherland's borders, Germans are expected to show their colors especially with respect to Germany's Nazi past. The public voice of Americans, in academia and in the media, is sometimes the voice of Jewish Americans who justifiably expect that one adopt a reflected attitude toward one's interlocutors. In addition, foreign residents in the United States must find a place in the complex web of "race" relations. This is particularly ironic for Germans, since in the German language "Rasse" is a completely discredited word, rendered unusable by its employment in Nazi terminology and now limited to distinctions between breeds of dogs. Any American application form, however, blithely asks me to identify myself as a member of the "white," or "Caucasian," race. Visa applications reserve a space for travelers to identify themselves if they participated in the activities of Nazi Germany between 1933 and 1945. American categories of identity, then, which highlight historical "correctness" (that is, ideological opposition to Germany's Nazi past), markers of race as well as possibly religion and class—these do not form part of visa applications, but they can be apparent from neighborhood stratifications—show me myself in a subject position—to borrow a term from literary theory—distinct from that of my youth, when everybody I knew was white, Catholic, middle-class, and mildly conservative.

My "attitude" toward Germany's Nazi past has become a test case for my political integrity in the country of which I am now a permanent resident. My explanations have elicited various responses from varying audiences. Specifically, a presentation on coming to terms with one's country's history will yield different results when given to an audience of white, Midwestern college students or, alternately, to an audience of African Americans—composed of students from Chicago's South Side and from the Deep South—at a historically black college in a Southern state. A person's cultural and political identity gains relevance only in context. What emerges from my comparison of the two presentations is a personal lesson about the public nature of one's beliefs and one's identity. Awareness of intercultural dynamics is, then, not a luxury made requisite only by the contemporary fascination with "culture" in American public discourse. Such awareness, rather, is a necessity, perhaps especially for a person who was socialized in highly homogeneous circumstances.

Like Voltaire's Candide—the optimistic student of Pangloss, who thought that intercultural competence could safely be navigated in the realm of ideas—I grew up in Westphalia. *Candide* is an object lesson for our time. Without detracting from Voltaire's genius, I might well call *Candide* the multicultural manifesto of the Enlightenment. The eponymous protagonist experiences senseless war, gains and loses a fortune, travels to all corners of the known world, meets Jesuits and papal inquisitors, and retires to a private enclave with a motley crew of companions from different walks of life to cultivate a common garden. Many ideals of the Enlightenment, such as tolerance, reason, and belief in happiness, have again gained currency in our day, possibly because of the fatal consequences of a rampant Romanticism that moves without stopping from Wagner and Nietzsche to Hitler. But even if reason can make a garden of our planet, we can no longer envision private enclaves for the like-minded. People of the twenty-first century need to move between gardens.

My education in the Westphalian public grammar school in the 1970s was progressive. Much to the dismay of our parents, my schoolmates and I read living East German authors instead of Goethe and Schiller. We learned three foreign tongues, thus imitating Pangloss more than Candide. We were perhaps the first generation of schoolchildren to be informed in full about the origins, events, and consequences of Germany's thirteen years under Nazi rule. Prosperity, security within the Western alliance, and the regaining of international respect for Germany were the catchwords of the day. In many ways, however, this education was theoretical: for all the good things I learned about Judaism, I never met a Jew.

The first test of my multicultural competence occurred when I became a graduate student at a large, well-known American university on the east coast. Many of my fellow graduate students, professors, and advisors were Jews. Many of the authors we studied were Jewish. Suddenly, the theory of Germany's collective guilt—which I had discarded—seemed somehow to apply to me. As the token German in many classes, I would frequently be called upon to explain my country's history and its subsequent developments. Over time, I was able to develop a defensible argument: born in 1960, I could clearly not take personal responsibility for any event that happened between 1933 and 1945, yet as a historically conscious German, I would forever be called, by the burden of my country's history, into responsibility for those suffering from persecution. "Never Again" was to be the uncomfortable motto for a moral imperative over my life.

I had developed my argument without taking into account the multiplicity of ethnic and racial experiences in the United States. As I turned from student to teacher, I soon found occasion to reexamine my stance. The small, Midwestern college at which I now teach requires all freshmen to enroll in a year-long class in the "Western Intellectual and Literary Tradition." My colleagues and I decided that I would give a lecture to the entire freshman class on my coming to terms with my country's history. As I explained German history of the twentieth century—the Weimar Republic, the rise of the Nazis, their political machinery, German compliance and isolated resistance—and as I finally recalled how a visit to Auschwitz I made as a student left me speechless for days, the reaction in the culturally homogeneous audience was predictable: shock, horror, and empathy. There are relatively few Jews in southwest Missouri. My white audience, not predisposed to any particular sentiment toward Jews, evinced the standard shock that any of us would feel in the presence of human suffering. My students perceived the lecture essentially as an academic learning experience, perhaps somewhat intensified by the unusual nature of the lecturer. Still, by comparison with, say, a concentration camp survivor, I am extremely far removed from the subject I discuss.

A few months later, I was invited to give the same presentation to the freshman class at a historically black college in the Deep South. A small but articulate minority of both Palestinian and African American students challenged me on my portrayal of the Jews as victims. To these students' thinking, my arguments were hopelessly mired in the past. As Blacks and Muslims living in the United States at the present time, they felt strong sympathies with the Palestinians against the Jewish state, and they quickly equated Israel's treatment of the occupied territories with the Nazis' persecution of the Jews. American inner cities and their Black population, they argued, suffer to this day from Jewish financial and commercial interests. How could I as a German defend the Jews when my forebears had reacted to perceived injustices similar to those many Blacks suffer today in the United States? Clearly, these students had a cultural learning experience that turned my presentation from an academic lesson into an invitation to react. To my German sentiment, the Holocaust means guilt and grave moral discomfort. To my audience, the Holocaust was one event in an ongoing series of clashes between culture groups, one of which defines itself largely by ideological opposition to the state of Israel.

All of a sudden, my comfortable theory had exploded. My naive belief that victimized groups—Jews in Nazi Germany, Blacks in the United States—feel solidarity with each other was no longer justified. As our discussion continued, I momentarily found myself taking a perverse kind of comfort in the position of victim—a completely new experience. Had I not felt before the unfairness in world opinion? Were not Germans, at home and abroad, held to a higher standard than anyone else? When a punk in Frankfurt roughs up a Turkish guest worker, does not the world press erupt in indignation, whereas a British skinhead attacking a Pakistani hardly achieves even local notoriety?

On further reflection, these thoughts turned out not to be productive. Their inaccuracy lies in the comparison of two unequal situations. The nature of evil is such that each occurrence must be measured by its own standard. One evil cannot necessarily be "put into perspective" by comparison to another one. The Holocaust does not become justifiable by the fact that other atrocities have been committed by other people at other times. Evil can also be transpersonal (e.g., in the spreading of an epidemic disease), but guilt and responsibility are personal. Thus, while there is no collective guilt, there is also no collective innocence.

The realm of intercultural negotiations needs to be approached differently. It is a matter of personal engagement. The proposals I shall now put forward are based on my experience as a teacher. The examples which sparked the proposals are personal in nature, yet I do not claim to have addressed their subject matter in full. While the immediate occasion for the different reactions I received in response to my lecture was a discussion of German history and the Holocaust, this essay is not the place to do justice to the gravity of that topic. Rather, I claim so grave a topic in order to remove from this essay any suspicion of frivolousness, straightforward though my proposals may appear to be.

First, an intercultural society needs to be educated in the culture of debate. I envision a truly civilized form of debate, in which listening skills become part of the rhetorical toolbox. The McLaughlin Group is hardly a model here. Instead, a cultured debate would take place among equals whose intention is not necessarily to convince one another, but whose commonality lies in their willingness to learn about different perspectives on the same question. The American tradition of rallying around the Constitution may be helpful here. To exemplify: if I brought the two student groups with whom I discussed German history into communication with each other, they would probably learn more about each other than about the topic at hand. As the "teacher" fades into the background, the process of intercultural debate has begun. At least for a time, participants in the debate would see the world from a different angle of vision and would consider respecting that alternative. Interestingly, a culture of debate is literally limitless. All participants, the "presenter" included, continually reexamine their stances. Far from being rampantly relativistic, the practice of continual reexamination is made necessary by the nature of multicultural debate. Since every participant is different, every participant deserves recognition. Understood in this manner, a multicultural existence is a philosophical existence: we ascribe to Socrates the adage that "the unexamined life is not worth living."

Second, an intercultural society needs to be polyglot. Primarily, this means competency in a foreign language. Arguments about language learning are legion, and many linguists can state them with more authority than this author. But in many ways, competency in a foreign language may only be the first step toward intercultural competence. That would also entail the ability to move between social classes or religious and ethnic groups and to act as "translator." Germans of my generation, for example, are generally quite comfortable communicating with their British and French and Spanish friends. But, as we learned recently, speaking with those of our compatriots who used to be East Germans is a different matter altogether. After forty years of separation, we share so few beliefs and concepts that we often doubt whether we speak the same language. Not only has the speech of West Germans become imbued with American idioms and that of East Germans with Russian idioms, but, more profoundly, the very understanding of national—or cultural—identity differs substantially. Allow me to simplify for the sake of clarity: West Germans, especially the thirty-something generation, have seen the only possible future for Germany in a European bond with strong transatlantic ties. We stressed European identity to the extent of neglecting German particularity. Through the sixties and seventies, our sense of national pride or patriotism—healthy or not—lay dormant. Only with the advent of the eighties and an increasing temporal distance from 1945 did we begin to sense a German identity. East Germans, on the other hand, stressed the fact that their country was "the first socialist state on German soil." In spite of their prominent place in the socialist brotherhood of nations, East Germans have some justification to the claim that they preserved a sense of German national identity. By chance, Weimar and Wittenberg came to be situated on the eastern side of the border. Yet the East Germans preserved their sense of national identity at the expense of virtually denying responsibility for Germany's Nazi past. The strength of the denial, and the burden of this particular past, were made apparent when the first freely elected East German parliament—before unification—opened its inaugural session with an apology to the state of Israel. So when we debate the role of Germany in the post-Cold War world or the possibility of a seat on the United Nations Security Council, we start from different points of view. In this debate, multicultural sensitivity supersedes the accidentals of language. Since the integration of the former East Germany into the West has in many ways turned out not to be a meeting between equals, but rather a process of absorption and refashioning in the Western image, a polyglot culture of debate will be required there for a long time to come. Third, education in such old-fashioned virtues as tolerance, politeness, and tact will contribute, I believe, to a better world culture. Optimism, Candide's specialty, will become a cherished commodity. A person's cultural identity, as I said above, is both a private and a public matter. If we want the public discourse to be productive, tolerance will be a more helpful approach than proselytism. "Tolerance" and "tact" may sound like easy subterfuges, but they take us back to the troubled eighteenth-century world of Candide, which Voltaire tried to meet with the tools of reason. In the practical, everyday world of multicultural encounters, tolerance and tact take on meaning at a surprising rate of speed. I would invite readers to test my proposals in their own lives.

The culture of debate, polyglot education, and the fostering of tolerance and tact are the ingredients of a well-defined and self-reflected identity. The three are interdependent as well: only persons sufficiently sure of themselves will face the world tolerantly. Any intercultural identity then, transatlantic or otherwise, will need to be, not sentimental, but rational.

Chapter 9

Chinese in America or Chinese-Americans: Building Multicultural Landscapes and Literacies

An Lan Jang

> Ethnic, gender, or class identities and symbolizations are most evident at their peripheries, where contacts with others evoke articulations and dramatizations of the self.
>
> —(White and Lutz)

When the forces of Chiang Kai-shek had to flee Mainland China in 1949, my father was appointed to a top position in promoting Mandarin Chinese and displacing Taiwanese as the official language in the province of Taiwan. I grew up with the tension of observing two Chinese languages competing for dominance and identity.

My father came from an old, highly educated, and wealthy Beijing family, and he tried to prevent all his children from learning Taiwanese. Although as a young person I admired many of my father's values, and even though Taiwanese was forbidden as public discourse (as for example in the schools), I of course learned Taiwanese in the streets. I noticed quite early in my life that the two languages called forth different senses of self and that these two selves and languages did not peacefully coexist. They competed inside of me, and the prize was "me." This experience of languages and "identity politics" initiated my interest in language and culture in conflict.

I want to talk about Chinese and English in the way these languages socially constructed conflict within me. I am not suggesting that the forms of language generate meaning, but that the *use* of such forms to argue a position, to explore a possibility, or to construct border identities are political actions involving language. Like Rey Chow, I am committed to setting up "oppositional discursive space" to help us negotiate our border identities democratically, with a minimum of oppressive influences. Yet, as Salman Rushdie has said, "We are increasingly becoming a world of migrants, made up of bits and fragments from here, there. We are here. And we have never really left anywhere we have been" (114). Hence my interest in and commitment to multicultural literacies: to understand where I have come from, where I am, and what futures can be imagined and co-created. In this chapter I want to talk about documenting the politics of cultural practices, rather than pretending that the interpretation of cultures is a nonpolitical activity. Just as Marcus and Fischer and also Simon and Dippo have argued for a *critical anthropology* or a *critical ethnography,* I want to agree with Derrida that "all experience is the experience of meaning. Everything that appears to consciousness, everything that is for consciousness in general, is *meaning*. Meaning is the phenomenality of phenomenon" (30). What does it *mean* to be a Chinese in the United States, or a Chinese American?

I was enculturated in traditional Chinese values in a Taiwan that responded to the Cultural Revolution in Mainland China by worshipping Confucian ideals of devotion to family (father-husband), and culture (male leaders). As a child and teenager I uncritically accepted the officially sanctioned Confucian values because they seemed to promote a sense of shared fate and connectedness. Already as a middle school student I was becoming aware, through American movies and television, of an emphasis on individuality that looked interesting, even exciting—from a distance—but that seemed lonely, isolated, and destructive. I recall a neighbor referring to American families as "blood strangers who live under the same roof." At the time I did not see this as a cultural stereotype, but as an insightful comment that helped me "understand" American culture. The "self" I was taught to be was very different.

Brian Morris (1994) describes the Confucian self this way: "The Chinese concept of the self has been seen as essentially sociocentric, as oriented towards significant others, and as involving self-development within a social context" (96). The central Confucian concept and general nearly all-purpose virtue, *jen*, which my teachers endlessly reiterated and paraphrased as "you have to live within the society"; "you have to get along with others"; "you have to fit in" were behaviors to be learned by heart, not explored or analyzed.

The character for *jen* looks like this: 仁. It is composed of two radicals or constituent parts: the "person" radical: 人, and the "two" radical: 二. The literal meaning of *jen* is "two people" or "double persons." The connotation of *jen* is that one should treat others as oneself and that personal actions should not be built on selfish or individual motivation. The well-being of the family or group must always be put first.

My high school and college teachers in Taiwan passed on to us a *jen* shrunk to mere ideological stereotype. They never mentioned that *jen* is an incredibly slippery or ambiguous term. Tu Wei-ming calls *jen* "discouragingly complex" (48). Hall and Ames emphasize that

> Whatever *jen* might mean for Confucius, several things can be said about it with reasonable certainty. First, it has a central role in the *Analects*, occurring some 105 times in fifty-eight of the 499 passages included in that text. Followers ask Confucius specifically about this concept more than any other (111).

Two paragraphs later, Hall and Ames add that much "of the problem in interpreting the *Analects*...arises from the fact that *jen* is at times used in its pre-Confucian 'particularistic' sense, and at other times used as general virtue" (111). I would have loved a sociolinguistic analysis of the different uses of the word, but even my requests for background information were turned away unanswered by teachers: "That question is not helpful or useful." I, of course, soon stopped asking questions.

The Taiwan government's use of Confucius as cultural scripture is consonant with Confucian tradition and China's long and dark political history:

> Thinking per se always involves a grounding in tradition and may never be modeled after the direct investigation of "nature" or undisciplined, imaginative constructions.
>
> For Confucius, knowledge is grounded in the language, customs, and institutions that comprise culture. Culture is the given world. Thinking is cultural articulation that renders this givenness effective....
>
> Confucius is, in fact,...a cultural positivist.
>
> That is to say, he is one who posits the received cultural tradition as the authority sine qua non for all knowledge and conduct (Hall and Ames, 67).

The Taiwan government's drastic commodification of an already traditionally hegemonic *jen* was the most palpable feature of the culture I was born into and remained in until the age of twenty-eight. Billboards of slogans filled the visual landscape, and formal education involved little more than rote learning of propaganda. I was able to begin a counterreading of the political propaganda at an early age because of the influence and ethos of my parents.

My father is a monarchist and for that reason he never joined the ruling party in Taiwan, the Kuomintang. He paid a high price for this in terms of career nonadvancement and the perpetual suspicion that he was secretly antigovernment.

My mother, with a university education in the desperate China of the 1930s, caught between the Chinese Civil War and the Japanese invasion, was a utopian thinker along Taoist anarchist lines (Morris 1981), a position she of course never communicated outside of the home. She was an inspiration to me, with a career of her own as an enlightened educator. She was an enabling parent and what we would now call a liberated woman. She contested my father's imperial patriarchy at every given point. Her mother, who lived with us for a time, had bound feet, and so could not move very well. My grandmother, though from a rich background, was illiterate: bound mentally as well as physically. Once, when I was ten, my grandmother saw me reading. She said to me: "You have 'big' feet. You can run and you can read. I can do nothing!" I looked at her not knowing what to say.

Twenty years later, as a then recent immigrant to the United States and a graduate student, I remembered my grandmother's sense of being circumscribed. As a woman and a minority, I felt my position was even worse than in Taiwan because there my only disadvantage was being a woman. In the United States I had a double disadvantage as female and minority. I quickly was made to see that feminism was for middle-class white women (hooks). My graduate program in the Teaching of English as a Second Language was composed almost entirely of white women.

In graduate school I worked extremely hard and became fiercely competitive. This was the apparent end of the collaborative orientation toward group life that the Confucian *jen* had constructed within me. In Taiwan, in school and college, no one volunteered answers or comments for fear of making fellow students feel less adequate. Such individual initiative would be viewed as "showing off." I am not saying there was no jealousy and competition, but such values and behavior were not socially affirmed by teachers and leaders. We studied together inordinately long hours because of our own initiative, we thought, and took pleasure in the examination results of peers. On the matter of cooperation, a Confucian quotation—used as mere slogan—was repeated endlessly by teachers: "Strong students should help the weaker ones." In what felt like a drastic, earthquake-like change, in the American graduate program I was isolated and came to feel that the only way to be the equal of white females was to excel them. Gone were the days of studying together and shared fate. My competitive attitude was my response to internalized racism and colonialism, which I did not entirely recognize at the time. Although China was never colonized through complete territorial occupation, yet, as Chow puts it:

> *in spite of* and perhaps because of the fact that it remained in many cases "territorially independent," it offers even better illustrations of how imperialism works—i.e., how imperialism as ideological domination succeeds best without physical coercion, without actually capturing the body and the land (8).

When I competed with the white female graduate students for grades, and they became resentful of my straight-A average, my internalized racism surfaced with a vengeance. They thought that they—as native speakers and possessors of mainstream American culture—had inherited the sole right to teach English as a second language and thus "American culture." I was viewed as an intruder, who, as a straight-A student, constituted a genuine threat in the small job market that they regarded as their private domain, and thus they saw me as an intellectual migrant worker who might take "their" job.

My response to this overt cultural-economic warfare—similar to what I had seen between Taiwanese Chinese and Mainland Chinese in Taiwan—was to affirm that the United States is a nation of immigrants and that I was here legally and therefore had equal rights and dignity. In Taiwan, I was a passive recipient of the benefits of being part of the elite Mainland social class that dominated Taiwan. But in the United States, as a Chinese woman, I was a double minority in a white-dominated society. I felt that the only way I could survive or fight back against white racism was to make "them" feel inferior as I had been made to feel. In order to do so, I had to, in a sense, *become* a racist: to outdo the whites at their own game. I became the "dangerous Other" they saw me as. I wanted to make them feel inferior by excelling them academically and in the long run economically. Considering how little an ESL teacher makes, we were foolishly fighting over the economic crumbs (of superficial) cultural pluralism.

At this point I struggled over whether I wanted to be a "Chinese in America" or a Chinese American, a deep issue for the Chinese in this country. David Yen-ho Wu says of group identity that for

> centuries the meaning of being Chinese seemed simple and definite: a sense of belonging to a great civilization and performing properly according to the intellectual elites' norm of conduct.... The Chinese as a group traditionally believed that when a larger Chinese population arrived in the frontier land, Sinicization was the only possible course. It was inconceivable that any Chinese could be acculturated by the inferior non-Chinese "barbarians"; however, such acculturation has been a common course of development for Chinese in the frontier land and overseas, although people still insist that an unadulterated Chinese culture is maintained by the Chinese migrants (176).

It was just at this time that I had to face the grueling issue of whether I would become a citizen of the United States and thus be obliged to renounce Chinese citizenship, or would I remain a permanent resident of the United States and thus maintain my Chinese nationality. Of course I felt, on several levels, that giving up my Chinese citizenship was giving up my Chinese identity. I finally decided that my loyalty was to Chinese culture and its possible permutations, not to the nation-states on either side of the Taiwan Straits.

The differences between being a Chinese in America and a Chinese American are profound. Did I see myself as a sojourner who would one day return to China? Did I want something in the United States that I would, after obtaining, "take home to China"? Or, would I put down roots and become a Chinese American? Finally I had to admit that my life was tied to the political possibilities I envisioned in a (potentially) multicultural democracy in the United States. I really have become a Chinese American. I have dual loyalty: to Chinese culture and its possible permutations and to the political entity, the United States, and to its possible political transformations.

I am committed to helping construct multicultural landscapes and literacies. A multicultural landscape is not a mere cultural theme park, superficial and insubstantial. It is a place of genuine oppositional discursive space where people can *agree* to disagree (the commonality) and to remain open to a succeeding array of unassimilated others (cultural pluralism). If monoculturalism is celebrating the self, then multiculturalism is celebrating the other.

A multicultural landscape is a place of dialogue and conversation. It is the opposite of a monocultural landscape in which patriarchal monologues are created by leaders and experts, while everyone else is supposed to look on in awe, as the speeding expert makes spurious claims to objectivity, a situation which is inherently undemocratic (Sampson).

But there is a dilemma. If a multicultural landscape doesn't have unassimilated others, then conditions of colonialism are at work. If there are unassimilated others, then our apparent multicultural landscape can be considered to be composed of monocultural groups: separate, alone, discrete. There are a series of monologues, but no real dialogues. I argue, therefore, that the only *fully* multicultural landscape is one in which symbolic and literal marriages between cultures take place.

Mixed-race children and genuinely multicultural constructions that are the creations of marriage, not rape, prostitution, or concubinage, represent a consciousness in which a self and other can freely interchange. For the multicultural child, the "other" is not assimilated in that she can play, for example, the Chinese "other" to the Anglo "self," and vice versa. The potential, here, for heteroglossia, for multifaceted selves that avoid oppressive structures and responses, led W. Maurice Shipley, in his contribution to this book, to write that

> ...discussions of "multiculturalism" and "diversity" cause me significant uneasiness because, as a Black man in America, I'd like to believe that my color has never been my problem. Inclusion has always been my goal—my dream. It seems to me that the same could be said of any ethnic group. For me the question remains: How do I get America to accept my being different—especially when it seems to be no real comfort to understand the value in differences? Every

> time I have to explain that difference, I think to myself: "They still don't get it." And now, I wonder as I look over to my little mulatto grandson, whose smile is both my joy and my hope—how do I change...his world, and make of it all that his smile thinks it is?...

Genuinely multicultural landscapes can only become dialogical and democratic with the development of multicultural literacies (Macedo; Geertz 1988). Such literacies "will open up new worlds and identities and overcome...oppressive situations." Multicultural literacies are inherently ideological, since they are the sites of "tension between authority and power on the one hand and resistance and creativity on the other" (Street, 8).

Multicultural literacies involve multicultural practices and conceptions of reading and writing. Can children understand the need for multicultural literacy better than adults? I recently observed a four-year-old, mixed-race, bilingual child playing with two dolls in a day-care center. One doll was a stereotyped Chinese in formal dress; the other was a blue-eyed blond in shorts. The child, using books, was teaching Chinese to the blond and English to the Asian doll. She explained to each doll in both languages that to be able to talk to each other, they needed to be able to read both languages or else they would fight. As I listened to the child, the caregiver's radio reported on the disastrous results of multicultural marriages in the former Yugoslavia. The marriages fell victim in large numbers to the civil war; spouses "returned" to their ethnic groups. It was poignant to see the common sense of this child, so badly needed in an adult world of such savage monocultural provincialism.

In the *Analects* of Confucius, chapter 28.2, we have a reference to *jen*. "The person of *jen*, wanting to stand on his own feet, does so by helping others stand on theirs. He is enlarged by enlarging others" (my translation). The tragedy of our world is that the four-year-old child understood the simple message of this Confucian text better than adults. We adults have created the monoculturalism of ethnic cleansing and surplus populations, while she and children like her are creating our best hope for a multicultural future.

Works Cited

Chow, Rey. *Writing Diaspora: Tactics of Intervention in Contemporary Cultural Studies*. Bloomington: Indiana University Press, 1993.

Derrida, Jacques. *Positions*, trans. Alan Bass. Chicago: University of Chicago Press, 1981.

Geertz, Clifford. *Works and Lives: The Anthropologist as Author*. Stanford: Stanford University Press, 1988.

———. *After the Fact: Two Countries, Four Decades, One Anthropologist*. Cambridge: Harvard University Press, 1995.

Hall, David, and Roger Ames. *Thinking through Confucius*. Albany: State University of New York Press, 1987.

hooks, bell. *Ain't I a Woman? Black Women and Feminism*. Boston: South End Press, 1981.

Macedo, Donaldo. *Literacies of Power: What Americans Are Not Allowed to Know*. Boulder: Westview Press, 1994.

Marcus, George, and Michael Fischer. *Anthropology as Cultural Critique: An Experimental Moment in the Human Sciences*. Chicago: University of Chicago Press, 1986.

Morris, Brian. "Lao Tzu and Anarchism." *Anarchist Review* 42 (1981): 9-16.

———. "Is Anthropology Simply a Romantic Rebellion against the Enlightenment?" *Eastern Anthropology* 39 (1986): 359-64.

———. *Anthropology of the Self: The Individual in Cultural Perspective*. London: Pluto Press, 1994.

Olson, Gary. "The Social Scientist as Author: Clifford Geertz on Ethnography and Social Construction." *Journal of Advanced Composition* 11 (1991): 245-68.

Rushdie, Salman. Interview in *Newsletter on Intellectual Freedom* 38 (1989): 106-14.

Sampson, Edward. *Celebrating the Other: A Dialogic Account of Human Nature*. Boulder: Westview Press, 1993.

Simon, Roger, and Donald Dippo. "On Critical Ethnographic Work." *Anthropology and Education Quarterly* 17 (1986): 195-202.

Street, Brian, ed. *Cross-Cultural Approaches to Literacy*. Cambridge: Cambridge University Press, 1993.

Tu, Wei-ming. "*Jen* as a Living Metaphor in the Confucian Analects." *Philosophy East and West* 31 (1981): 45-54.

White, Geoffrey, and Catherine Lutz. Introduction. In Theodore Schwartz, Geoffrey White, and Catherine Lutz, eds. *New Directions in Psychological Anthropology*. Cambridge: Cambridge University Press, 1992.

Wu, David Yen-ho. "The Construction of Chinese and Non-Chinese Identities." *Daedalus* 120, no. 2 (1991): 159-79.

Chapter 10

The "Other" before Me: A Bicultural Dialogue

Solange de Azambuja Lira and Arnold Gordenstein

The Conquest of America: The Question of the Other, by Tzvetan Todorov, was published in French in 1982 and in English in 1984 by Harper and Row. Todorov argues that the sixteenth-century confrontation between the Spanish explorers and the Aztecs commenced a dialogue which has framed and energized much of Western social and political discourse from that time until the present and focuses our contemporary concerns regarding multiculturalism. The consequences of this historic discovery of the "other," Todorov writes, "heralds and established our present identity." Since the discovery was accidental, neither explorers nor natives could anticipate the people they would encounter, therefore the experience serves nearly as a laboratory model for the examination of an uncontaminated and unbiased "other." Todorov deals with the political, philosophical, and psychological dimensions of the interchange, examining the writings of Columbus and the events surrounding Cortez's experience in Mexico. He analyzes the writings of two remarkable priests, Diego Durán and Bernardino de Sahagún, who studied the culture of the Aztecs in order to convert them but, converting few, left the best books on the subject. Indeed, Sahagún flirted with heresy by publicly discussing the many parallels between Aztec religion and Christianity.

Both priests lived virtually their entire lives in Mexico, both employed different strategies, but neither could prevent the virtual extinction of the people they meant to protect and convert. Todorov explores the discovery of the "other" through the words of Columbus, Las Casas, Sepulveda, Durán and Sahagún, as well as the actions of Montezuma and Cortez. Since Columbus, Todorov writes, westerners "have discovered the totality of which they are a part, whereas hitherto they formed a part without a whole."

Since Todorov does not attempt to exhaust the discussion of "otherness" in all its aspects, the present dialogue addresses the way it infiltrates and influences a relationship between individuals of two cultures. The amplifications of the present conversation into cultural concerns, as well as the similarities between this encounter and one between members of any two cultures, should be clear to the careful reader.

A native of Rio de Janeiro, Solange de Azambuja Lira is an associate professor who works with language diversity issues.

Her husband, Massachusetts-born Arnold Gordenstein, is an associate professor who teaches American literature, minority literature, and Latin American literature.

For more than two decades they have spent about equal amounts of time between their two countries, teaching and raising their four children, three of whom were born in Brazil. All members of the family, with varying degrees of facility, are bilingual.

Arnold: So how should we begin? Any beginning is going to be artificial but I suppose the inescapable beginning is Todorov's description of the relationship between the explorers and the natives in the newly discovered lands.

Solange: Intruders, not explorers. New to the intruders.

Arnold: All right. New to the intruders. And once we've identified this relationship and tried to describe it, our job is going to be to find if these intruders' incredible experience of finding this unexpected place has any parallel in the more mundane relationship between individuals like you and me.

Solange: Keep the mundane to yourself. In fact I think you can keep much of this to yourself. Frankly, I think this is a mistake. I don't think this comparison is valid at all. You and I could never conceivably stand for the confrontation between the invading culture and the invaded one. If I didn't know you better I'd even say that was patronizing or borderline sexist. I was never invaded. I was willing. You were invited.

Arnold: I'll admit this might be the fiction writer or the literature professor at play. You know, Romeo and Juliet. Not just loving individuals. Warring clans. Love and hate on flip sides. Maybe you'll agree to that, for starters. We're symbols.

Solange: I've been called worse. But there are other reasons why this microcosm won't work. Even aside from the emotional level where I was never passive, when you reached my shore there was also the historical level. Though you were initially fairly ignorant of my culture, I was never ignorant of yours, neither experientially nor literally. In your solipsism you seem to forget that I lived in the U.S. as a child, that I studied American literature long before you even heard of Machado de Assis, and that I knew several Americans long before I knew you. And all of this helped me build up a bank of U.S. experience that I could draw on later. And because of it I could understand and even anticipate some of your reactions though you could anticipate very few of mine. This is nothing like Montezuma and Cortez, at least Todorov's Montezuma and Cortez. It might even be the reverse. We were more like the wise native and the naive explorer, which is not what Todorov described at all. I had a measure of control over the relationship—far larger than the original Americans had over the conquistadors. It's probably even colonialist to suppose that this third-world female was won over to a superior culture. I think our usefulness in illustrating Todorov is very limited. Certainly you have to agree with that.

Arnold: Not yet. We simply haven't found the right level of the comparison. How about this? I think even you would agree that there is a real economic disparity between our countries, which corresponds, in part, to the Todorov description. This disparity is there through no fault of yours or mine, but we do operate within our systems and we do take advantage of what we can. Cortez didn't invent the blunderbuss or import the horse from Africa, but he used them to his advantage as any sixteenth-century Spaniard would. So what I'm asking is do you think that the perception of a technological gap might have infiltrated our relationship the way it dominated the one Todorov describes? I think that's where Todorov begins to talk about us.

Solange: Are you suggesting that I went with you because you're a rich Gringo?

Arnold: Doesn't the female caribou go off to rut with the male who won the horn-bashing contest? And is it for more horn-bashing or is it because she has witnessed a demonstration that he will provide best for her offspring?

Solange: So you're saying I went with you because I anticipated that you and U.S. technological superiority would provide best for our eventual offspring?

Arnold: Look. I'm perfectly aware who's the major earner in this house but I'm not talking about my paltry pay. I'm talking about this culture's support system, which we're living in. That might be part of the reason why you edged toward me at the beginning.

Solange: Certainly never on a conscious level.

Arnold: Who's talking conscious? I'm only saying if we could re-create the emotional milieu of our earliest encounters we might find something that might correspond to the original explorers with the natives.

Solange: Even if you're right, that's only half of it. What about you and me aside from our cultures?

Arnold: From my side you often seemed to me exotic in our first years and maybe "exotic" is my word for "other." At least your Brazilian setting was always exotic to me. And to the extent that the setting characterized you, it was very positive and attractive.

Solange: Well, you were never exotic to me, if that's what you're fishing for. If I ever felt anything about your culture it was a mild distaste for North Americans' presumed superiority. In fact, I think it was crucial that you were willing to criticize your own culture, which made you less "other" and more reachable to me from the very beginning. I suppose I always wanted less otherness and more availability. And even if I did feel any otherness about you then I think the feeling has diminished as I've become comfortable in the U.S. I'm not positive that this is good news but I don't see that our contrasting cultures are dead-center of our relationship anyway. For that matter I still have to be convinced that our relationship on the most fundamental level is importantly different from that of any two individuals from anywhere doing the tough work of trying to create a joint life. Seems to me there's enough otherness in any relationship to go around. Besides, we're both "others" to each other in a whole variety of ways besides our countries. You're Jewish and I'm nominally Catholic. I grew up in the '50s and you in the '40s. These influences create otherness too. More important, I grew up in a major Latin American city and you in a small New England one. I can't think of a more othering process than that. My father was a colonel in a country that reveres the military. My mother was a schoolteacher. We had servants. Your father's father was from a Russian schtetl. Your mother was educated, but a housewife. We're "other" to one another in a whole array of ways.

Arnold: Sure, but are these equivalent to Todorov's "other"? For instance, I've come to think that Todorov's "other" is nearly what the nineteenth-century philosophers called the "not-me." That's supposed to distinguish ontologically between the subject—us—and the objects which comprise the natural world but it also includes all those "not-me" influences you just enumerated. I think that there are a whole series of "others," some personal and some social, and I think if this dialogue about the "other" is going to continue we have to adapt it to much larger parameters. For instance, when any two individuals face one another we have a confrontation with the "other." But the conflict between the sexes might be the "other" confrontation at its simplest human level, more fundamental even than the confrontation between explorer and native but containing the same dynamic.

Solange: Don't you think that your maleness might be leading you to think in terms of confrontation and conflict?

Arnold: That could be, but that doesn't get rid of the question. A lot of people are male. Furthermore, could it be that not all "others" can be reconciled or incorporated or whatever one finally does with "others"? I'm not even certain that the ultimate "other" confrontation might even be, finally, a chemical irreconcilability, molecule against molecule. If this is so, then perhaps the resolution of this relationship between two "others" comes simply to this: do the chemical reactions move us toward or move us away? Do we incorporate in order to increase or do we clash and diminish?

Solange: Aren't we going a little far afield here? What I'd really like us to talk about is how this concept of the "other" has affected our own bicultural relationship. That's complicated enough.

Arnold: All right, then. I think it affected us a lot at first, but a lot less now.

Solange: Are you saying that Brazil and I don't seem very exotic any more?

Arnold: Not much. The "other" perception has decreased with familiarity. By the way, I'm also not certain this is all bad. But I also wonder if you and I have actually changed or if my perception has changed because I know you and Brazil better. Then has it changed through education, through ordinary aging, through a relaxation of my defenses, or is it simply an overdue dose of reality?

Solange: Are you still talking Todorov?

Arnold: I'm still talking Todorov by focusing on the evolution of the "other" feeling in my life. What I'm saying is I went through a transition similar to that of the explorers, from sensing the exotic to feeling alienated.

Solange: Just now you've revealed your "other" better than I could have hoped. Because your otherness for me is very American. It's your self-centeredness, your ego, your self-indulgence, your distance, and the superior, rational coldness with which you defend them. You've just shown me all of that.

Arnold: Have you noticed whenever you want to be critical you reach back for national stereotypes? Whether they apply or not. Self-centered. Superior. Rational. Defining the "other" becomes almost the same thing as listing a culture's least lovely characteristics. But you may have something there, all the same. For what is "other" besides off-putting? That is, what makes us feel strange or alienated in the presence of the foreigner? Isn't that what "other" is?

Solange: How about positive? Doesn't the presence of all us foreigners in the house ever give you a positive thrill?

Arnold: Sure. I mentioned the exotic before and I still feel your exoticness sometimes even now and that makes the relationship an adventure and that is very positive. I've even come to think by now that a relationship with one of my compatriots might seem timid and almost incestuous. You don't behave like the Americans I know, and that's fine with me. You're more open. You're more susceptible. You carry your values on a placard. You're more willing to let your simplicity show. You're more devoted to happiness as a prime goal and value than an American would be.

Solange: You've described a Latin bimbo.

Arnold: Well, if I've described a Latin bimbo, you've described a Puritan prig.

Solange: I prefer the Latin bimbo.

Arnold: Obviously. But what we've just learned is that both of us harbor these secret, ominously negative stereotypes of the "other." But that should come as no surprise. There are times when I feel that my mate is not from another culture but from another planet altogether—no doubt you feel similar things—and these are distressing and lonely times. I sometimes feel like I've lost my old secure cultural identity and haven't fully gained a new one. Or is this what anyone in the world periodically feels?

Solange: It is, but I think it's complicated by the influences of our different cultures.

Arnold: Complicated in what ways?

Solange: Political ways.

Arnold: You're not talking "politics" politics. You're talking about what R. D. Laing called the politics of the family, aren't you?

Solange: Sure. We live—we all live—in at least two political systems and national politics is only one of them. The important one is the politics of your family. How the power is distributed among its members and where you stand in the chain. That's what prepares you for what we like to call the larger political world. Don't you agree?

Arnold: I agree, but it's even more complicated than that. I think our own personal politics are produced by a dialectic between the family and the national politics in which we matured. You have your political attitudes because you grew up under a national military dictatorship, in a colonel's house, within an extended Latin family and awoke in the time of the hippies. You were ripe for rebellion, for a commune. And your multicultural attitudes have a lot to do with that background. My profile is a lot less clear.

Solange: Not so. You're from a middle middle-class Jewish family, grew up during the Holocaust and just after the Depression. Your politics were as predetermined as mine. You had to be an old-fashioned crusading New Deal Democrat. Why you're practically pretelevision, sweetheart. There aren't many of you left. And talk about free will. You had as little choice as I did. Your background predisposed you to multiculturalism as much as mine did. It was no accident that you found a foreign mate. You probably even saw me as an oppressed minority like yourself. I only wonder what I saw in you through the "otherness" screen.

Arnold: You saw a high-tech caribou who won the horn-bashing contest. Remember him? To tell the truth, I find the inaccuracies in these perceptions of one another even more tantalizing and disturbing than the direct hits. For instance, compared to me, you were never a downtrodden minority. I might have regarded you as a downtrodden minority but you were from the ruling class in Brazil. You had 95 percent of the population below you, economically and politically. I mentioned the symbolism of us before, the Capulet and Montague of us. I think we saw a lot of symbolism in each other at first, and that's a lot of what the "other" is.

Solange: So you're saying that we may have come together because we both seriously misread one another? Is that what multiculturalism is in for? A series of mistakes, reading the symbols for the realities?

Arnold: It could be. But in our case I doubt if we've remained together because of any misreadings. Our relationship must have some genuine glue in it or it wouldn't have lasted so long. And the glue may even involve our biculturalism. The language use is important, and that's a political matter. Originally a barbarian was someone who didn't speak your language. Colonizers always insist on their own languages, not the language of the colonized. When an invader doesn't use the natives' language he's showing contempt. Even so, we spoke English at home while we lived in Brazil and we're trying to keep the Portuguese fluent now that we're here. And that's fundamental. Sahagún wrote a twelve-volume study of Aztec culture in Nahuatl, first, and Spanish, second. According to Todorov, he and Durán began the dialogue with the natives that we are struggling to revive today. Even Cortez spoke some Nahuatl and understood the Aztecs better than they understood him. How many of our multicultural teachers actually speak the languages of the cultures they're trying to bring in? And you'll notice that the American attitude, even at its best, always seems to be "join us." It's never "we'll join you."

Solange: So what's lost if you don't learn the language?

Arnold: Todorov gives a good example, and by the way, he's a Bulgarian who writes in French. He said that Nahuatl, the Aztec language, was designed to communicate between people and the earth, while European languages are mainly for people talking to people. In destroying Indian language, the whole habit of communicating with the earth was lost.

Solange: Obviously we've got to keep working on the languages.

Arnold: Obviously. And I may even live long enough to perfect my Portuguese. I envy the kids because they were born with their Portuguese and I've had to struggle to learn mine. But what I want to know is what else should we do? How should we proceed if we want to keep both cultures alive in the family?

Solange: How did the cultural explorers in Todorov's book proceed? Durán and Sahagún did it by studying the other culture and participating in it. By speaking the language and thinking in it and even emoting in it. By eating the food and changing their body rhythms and conversation patterns and, especially, by loving and hating in the language. Once you've learned another set of physical and emotional responses you can't be satisfied with only one.

Arnold: It occurs to me that what you've just said is going to look to the people reading this like a religious convert saying you can't visit God unless you kneel in my particular church or temple or mosque or shrine.

Solange: Face it. There is a temptation to view your own worldliness like a membership in an elite club. But what should really happen when you acquire a new culture is you see that some things that seemed absolute before are absolute no longer and you become more tolerant of new configurations and you begin to view the possibility of enlarging your own experience and your own capacity as a very exciting prospect.

Arnold: If you can work it out.

Solange: You don't think so?

Arnold: Did you notice that the more we talked, the more we found differentness, resistance, and antagonism in each other? And we have good will for one another. So did Cortez and Montezuma finally work it out? The Duráns and Sahagúns are only footnotes to the bloody, horrible story of Cortez in Mexico. You would think that his understanding of the Aztecs should have prevented him from destroying them, but it didn't. So I'm not convinced that sympathy for another culture leads to its preservation. It might even lead to that loneliness I mentioned before. Now consider it on a national scale. Millions of people who had lost their old cultures and hadn't yet gained new ones. The process might be very painful and widespread, there would be no turning back and divorces aren't possible between cultures. And who knows what kind of political climate that amount of angst would produce? If this is interweaving we're talking about I think its problems have been importantly underestimated. What was it Ike McCaslin said in Faulkner's *Go Down, Moses?* Not yet, not yet. Maybe in a thousand years, but not yet. Am I, two whole generations after the pogroms, entirely free from the habit of racial thinking? Or have the African-Americans, who have been here three centuries longer than my family has, finally become woven into the fabric of American society? I'm not at all convinced that a workable interweaving will take place in the next centuries, if it's interweaving we want. I can't imagine people giving up what held them together for millennia and I'm not even sure, on balance, it's a good idea if they did.

Solange: Let me ask you something. Do you still consider yourself an American?

Arnold: I suppose so, but in a wholly different spirit from previously. I'm much more willing to admit America's faults now.

Solange: I hadn't noticed. So do you consider yourself an American?

Arnold: Do you consider yourself a Brazilian?

Solange: Sure. Forever. But do you?

Arnold: You know, I've considered switching allegiances. I think I'm capable of doing so, once I find a perfect society somewhere. Yeah, I'm an American, and rather proud of it, though I have serious trouble relating to a lot of the culture of the 1990s—the booklessness, the violence, the loss of cordiality. What I used to think of as a neighborhood feeling all across the land.

Solange: Then there you have it. That's what's holding multiculturalism back.

Arnold: You mean nationalism?

Solange: Call it national sentiment, which is necessarily backwards-looking. The force that makes otherwise rational adults cheer their heads off for the national team in the World Cup.

Arnold: How do you think our kids feel about their two cultures? Have we left them a burden or a gift?

Solange: I hope Brazil never faces the U.S. in a World Cup final, if that's what you mean. Maybe it would be better simply to ask if they love people in both places and if their cells vibrate equally in both settings. I'm not talking on a logistical level of course. They'll have to figure out where to spend their time and what to love. But I'm certain they think and feel in two cultures far more effortlessly than we do.

Arnold: No question of it. They are the future.

Solange: I agree.

Arnold: If you do, it will be the first time. And you also got in the last word.

Solange: Did I?

Arnold: Yes, I said yes you did, yes.

Afterword: The Complex Dynamics of Multiculturalism

Robert Eddy

I

> Approaching the third millennium, we are at the point of transition from...Modernity to Post-Modernity. Placed at this transition by changes beyond our control, we have a choice between two attitudes toward the future, each with its own "horizons of expectation." We may welcome a prospect that offers new possibilities, but demands novel ideas and more adaptive institutions; and we may see this transition as a reason for hope, seeking only to be clearer about the novel possibilities and demands involved in a world of practical philosophy, multidisciplinary sciences, and transnational or subnational institutions. Or we may turn our backs to the promises of the new period, in trepidation, hoping that the modes of life and thought typical of the age of stability and nationhood may survive at least for our lifetimes.... These two attitudes to the future—one of imagination, the other of nostalgia—do

> not imply different horizons of expectation.
> The choice is one between facing the future,
> and so asking about the "futuribles" open to us,
> or *backing into* it with no such horizons or ideas.
> —Stephen Toulmin

Some Americans welcome multiculturalism, and others deplore it. No one, however, can dismiss it as irrelevant to the most fundamental political issues which will determine the shape of the United States in the twenty-first century. What is multiculturalism? My short answer is this: multiculturalism is an openness to unassimilated otherness.

Multiculturalism involves uncovering and then judging all the dimensions of our being as cultural constructs. Multiculturalism posits that we are inextricably in the midst of a shared fate in the twenty-first century. Salman Rushdie has written that we "are increasingly becoming a world of migrants, made up of bits and fragments from here, there. We are here. And we have never really left anywhere we have been" (114).

We live in intercultural spaces and borderlands with plural identities and fluid selves, and too many of us are not comfortable with this newer reality. We want to regain monocultural simplicity and the security of oversimplifying our identities and therefore our responsibilities for one another. But as Julia Kristeva has said, "the foreigner is within me, hence we are all foreigners" (192). We are trying to run from the overwhelming reality that if "we are all foreigners," then our identities and connections are ineluctable.

The above quotation is from Kristeva's provocatively titled book *Strangers to Ourselves*. We need to see the dialogical nature of the temporary intersections we call "self," which are formed from the transitory congruence of voices we internalize from the many others with whom we share and have shared human experience. If there is no essence or core self, if our self is something we create from the options, concepts, and practices made available by our culture(s), then it is profoundly and simply true that we need each other to bring into being possibilities for growth and creativity which further personal and social transformation, the re-imagining of self and the world.

Some would grandly label our interconnectedness "Gaia," that sacerdotal, environmentalist, pantheistic sense that we are all one. Others consider multiculturalism a demographic shotgun wedding. Still others deny our interdependence with a frigid sense of the isolated self. I submit that there are no more human islands left, whether individuals or groups.

Here it is helpful to see the connection of multiculturalism with the contemporary science of chaos. This is a valuable context in which to converse about the theory and practical issues of multiculturalism because it helps us to see the relationships between order and disorder. If, as the science of chaos demonstrates, order and disorder are not opposites, then change, disruption, disputes, and even disasters can be seen as natural and inevitable characteristics of all complex systems. Of course "scientific results cannot be equated with social programs" (Hayles, 15) in any simpleminded way, but we need to prepare for these disorderly events rather than trying to design them away completely, which appears to be impossible.

What is the best way to prepare for multicultural disorders and even disasters? Surely the most important point is to recognize our shared fate. The planetary technological rhythms and the chaotic agitations of our setting will not admit the continuation of an adolescent sense of separation and frontier mentality. We are the frontier. Not one giant self, but a series of strange attractors. Chaos studies has demonstrated that the glyph or sigil called a "Strange Attractor" is widely applicable to analyses of patterns of change and accidents in complex systems. The strange attractor represents "any point of a system's cycle that seems to attract the system to it" (Hayles, 8). Hayles explains that chaotic systems

> are more common in nature than ordered systems.... The pervasiveness of strange attractors was both exhilarating and puzzling—exhilarating because it suggested that the idea had a wide scope; puzzling because it implied that systems that seemed completely different from one another nevertheless had something in common (9, 10).

What happens if we think of multicultural patterns, the tendency of multicultural ideas to cohere in meaning, as a series of strange attractors? Perhaps, according to the ordered disorder science has demonstrated in chaos studies, we might all be strange attractors—centers of intercultural magnetism and creativity—for ten minutes in the new multicultural setting of the twenty-first century. Thus, the strange attractor might put an interesting twist on Andy Warhol's quip about us all being famous for fifteen minutes in the future. I will draw out some of the crucial implications of chaos studies for multiculturalism at the close of this afterword.

The dance of plural identities must be the art form of the twenty-first century. In exchange for the loss of a microscopic singular self, impermeable and absolute unto death, indeed eternity, we have a cosmic dance of strange attractors and potentially endless creativity and productiveness—anything is possible except a permanent, changeless self; that prison is gone the way of the physical frontier.

Since the new multicultural setting is pushing people away from singular identities, we are all being displaced, and a politics of displacement is upon us. Such a politics resists "novel ideas and more adaptive institutions," as Stephen Toulmin mentions in the headnote, and is fraught with great danger, as seen in Rwanda or the former Yugoslavia, with their nightmare visions of ethnic cleansing and genocide, a way to end the world without the bomb.

Certainly the loss of cultural roots can be a profoundly disturbing experience. In the postmodern world such a loss often leads to mindless aggression against the "Other," which is really a projection of and an attack upon the newer self one must, but is reluctant to, become. Yes, it is understandable that one will tend—at least occasionally, and sometimes compulsively—to long for one's displaced or stereotypically simple self. But such nostalgia (especially for the control it implies) should not be the basis for our politics. The incurable intolerance the people of Rwanda or of the former Yugoslavia express toward each other is both a nightmare vision and a dreadful reality, but it is also a possible symbol of the twenty-first century, and must be overcome by our glimpsing broader and interconnected horizons.

Multiculturalism will surely become an increasingly politicized and emotional subject as we near the point in the coming decades when the United States becomes a white-minority country. Let us not pretend that the national situation is anything other than serious. We would be playing a dangerous game if we thought it was only in other parts of the globe that nightmare scenarios of ethnic warfare can occur. David Rieff warned us in 1993 that it is not only in the former Yugoslavia—a multiculturalist's nightmare—that a multicultural society "is steadily becoming less democratic, less just, and more impoverished" (72). It will require the best that is in us, individually and collectively, if we are to evolve as a democratizing society.

II

> If wandering, considered as a state of detachment from every given point in space, is the conceptual opposite of attachment to any point, then the sociological form of "the stranger" presents the synthesis, as it were, of both of these properties.... The stranger will thus not be considered here in the usual sense of the term, as the wanderer who comes today and goes tomorrow, but rather as the man who comes today and stays tomorrow—the potential wanderer, so to speak, who, although he has gone no further, has not quite got over the freedom of coming and going. He is fixed within a certain spacial circle—or within a group whose boundaries are analogous to spacial boundaries—but his position within it is fundamentally affected by the fact that he does not belong in it initially and that he brings qualities into it that are not, and cannot be, indigenous to it.
>
> —Georg Simmel

Amy Guttman has reminded us that "respectable moral disagreements...call for deliberation, not denunciation" (Taylor,

22). To try to remain open or to open up, requires us to see the stranger as not absolutely other. In a noncolonizing, nonpatronizing relation, we must see those with whom we seriously differ or disagree as representing a position we are willing to countenance if the argument and evidence are sufficiently convincing. This openness to unassimilated otherness is not a standardless relativism, but instead an acknowledgment of the dialogical character of the social construction of the self, especially in the case of multicultural woman or man. But what is the nature and where is the site of this multicultural exchange?

The site of multiculturalism is the intercultural experience of a dialogical landscape. This landscape and experience are highly concrete; Mikhail Bakhtin would call this place the chronotope, where "time and space are utterly interdependent." Entry "into the sphere of meaning is accomplished only through the gates of the chronotope, which produces pictures of timed-places and placed-times" (Folch-Serra, 274).

Bakhtin helps us to see that the multicultural self is never whole; it is always becoming. He writes that "a locality is the trace of an event, a trace of what had shaped it" (189). He explains that "the contingency that governs events is inseparably tied up with space, measured primarily by *distance* on the one hand and by *proximity* on the other" (99). When dissonance occurs in the dialogical landscape of multiculturalism, we could call it culture shock. In this experience of serious inharmony, we are "distant" from our home or first culture and "proximate" to our host or second culture. We are in effect between two cultural worlds. Our choices in this high-stress situation appear to be merely binary: either/or. We could try to become monocultural again and burrow ourselves in a monologue. But this doesn't work very well because it gives the lie to the complexity of the reality in front of us and also within us. It is only the fundamentalist impulse that can blink away the complexity and contingency of the dialogical landscape. The fundamentalist response is to cut the ground away from all others in the dialogical landscape and retreat to an idealized past that never existed: an absolute monologue where all other voices are silenced absolutely.

A dialogical response to the complexities of a multicultural experience, especially when culture shock is present—as it always is to some degree at least—is indeed the opposite of the fundamentalist response of silencing the dissonant voice. Dialogicalism celebrates the other as the dimension of self that has until now remained the stranger, an unrealized potential. In dialogue with the stranger, the other, those who are different, we contest, clarify, and construct our newer and developing senses of self.

Each culture, at any given point in time, has a dominant narrative of what it means to be a member of that group. This narrative provides individuals with what Appiah calls "scripts," roles which they can play within the culture to give meaning to their lives. But, Appiah reminds us,

> crossculturally it matters to people that their lives have a certain narrative unity; they want to be able to tell a story of their lives that makes sense. The story—my story—should cohere in the way appropriate by the standards made available in my culture to a person of my identity (160).

If cultures provide the scripts of our lives, does that mean multicultural men and women can create any identity they want?

> Authenticity speaks of the real self buried in there, the self one has to dig out and express. It is only later, in reaction to Romanticism, that the idea develops that a self is something that one creates, makes up, so that every life should be an art work whose creator is, in some sense, his or her own greatest creation. (This is an idea one of whose sources, I suppose, is Oscar Wilde.)
>
> Of course, neither the picture in which there is just an authentic nugget of selfhood, the core that is distinctively me, waiting to be dug out, nor the notion that I can simply make up any self I choose, should tempt us. We make

> up our selves from a tool kit of options made available by our culture and society. We do make choices, but we do not determine the options among which we choose (155).

The immense value of being multicultural is that each of our constituent cultures provides choices, which, when combined, create more options than either tradition or assimilation alone.

On this very point of multicultural settings creating new life scripts, Robert Hughes, in *Culture of Complaint: The Fraying of America,* reminds us that "America is a construction of mind, not of race or inherited class or ancestral territory"(12). America is an intercultural space which through gradual transformation and sometimes chaotic perturbation is trying to achieve true multiculturalism. The culture wars of contemporary America can best be defined as the resistance of the various forms of hermetically sealed group consciousness to the openness, uncertainty, and dialogical methodology required by multiculturalism. Each culture is always already political; it inherently desires to universalize its point of view. As Hughes puts it, "If someone agrees with us about the aims and uses of culture, we think him objective; if not, we accuse him of politicizing the debate" (60).

The dialogical methodology of multiculturalism requires us to understand that even when a majority culture does not fear that it will be transformed out of existence by contact with other cultures, even in such a condition of stability, it can continue to preserve its "vitality only through an unrestrained revisionism, by sketching out alternatives to the status quo or by integrating alien impulses—even to the point of breaking with its own traditions" (Habermas, 131). Only the dialogical method of multiculturalism can assure us that we are not talking to ourselves in a monologue which has lost all contact with the complexity of democratic practices. What happens in a dialogue with other people? We talk, listen, argue, agree, disagree, negotiate, compromise, ask questions, provide answers, describe, explain, tell stories, praise, promise, laugh, and cry (Sampson, 97). What are the key features of the dialogical method? Sampson lists four: 1) Dialogues happen between people. We cannot know what happened by talking to any one person. 2) Dialogues are public. Since they are not personal or private, they use "a system of signs" that are shared and understood by the participants. 3) Dialogues "involve addressivity." They are conversations among specific people "in a specific situation" to achieve definite social ends. 4) Dialogues "encompass verbal, nonverbal, symbolic and written material" (97). Sampson emphasizes that since we are dialogical beings, all "that is central to human nature and human life—and here I mean mind, self, and society itself—is to be found in processes that occur between people in the public world of our everyday lives" (98). What is the goal of this dialogical celebration of the other? Congruence.

The goal of multiculturalism should be congruence. As I use the term, congruence refers to the "resonance of a number of cultural patterns" (Lewis and Jungman, xxiii). This resonance represents the optimum harmony potentially present in any multicultural landscape. The seeking of congruence could be dismissed as utopian, but, as a goal, it is a rational and democratic alternative to perpetual conflict. Congruence, which can happen on the individual level, can also be the goal of groups. The key point, however, is that congruence, certainly of a permanent kind, is a necessarily unreachable goal, a useful fiction. "Permanent congruence," as any absolute system, would be totalizing and oppressive. It would be a reinvention of oppressive community and a master narrative. It would be an attempt to silence the multitude of other voices that is the life of multiculturalism.

Why should we have congruence as a goal if it is both unreachable and, even if it could be reached, would constitute an oppressive structure? If congruence represents the optimum harmony potentially present in any multicultural landscape, and if the multicultural landscape is always subject to chaotic perturbation, and thus the landscape is always changing, sometimes drastically, then our structures of congruence must also change in a fluid and open manner. Do these continuing changes make a permanent goal any less worthy of pursuit by a democratizing society?

III

> One of the oddities of the situation is that the assault on the Western tradition is conducted very largely with analytical weapons forged in the West. What are the names invoked by the coalition of latter-day Marxists, deconstructionists, poststructuralists, radical feminists, Afro-centrists? Marx, Nietzsche, Gramsci, Derrida, Foucault, Lacan, Sartre, de Beauvoir, Habermas, the Frankfurt "critical theory" school—Europeans all. The "unmasking," "demythologizing," "decanonizing," "dehegemonizing" blitz against Western culture depends on methods of critical analysis unique to the West—which surely testifies to the internally redemptive potentialities of the Western tradition.
>
> —Arthur M. Schlesinger, Jr.

Thus, multiculturalism is not an either/or issue. If we let it become that, we have already caved in to ethnocentrism. It should not be a question of male, Eurocentric Western Civilization versus minority or other cultural worlds. It should be a question of both/and, of intersubjectivity, of how to achieve true communication across large communicative distances. We need to study and inhabit conceptual frontiers and intercultural spaces.

Although different voices in the United States will disagree about the extent of the multicultural conversations, most will agree that there has been some progress in democratizing border crossings involving race, ethnicity, and gender. But what about social class? Here we have our most serious challenge to multiculturalism. Even as non-radical a commentator as Haynes Johnson insists that in the "expanding underclass exists a world that the middle class of all races and ethnicities deals with from a distance, and with scant understanding" (237).

At the time when it is most seriously needed, public higher education, which functions in part to ameliorate class divisions, is shrinking instead of expanding. Moreover, since the cost of a community college education, to give but one example, is skyrocketing (Gitlin, 30), we seem to be in the midst not of a war against poverty but against the poor (Wacquant). Our prisons are overflowing.

What happens if we subject the deepening poverty in the United States to the methodology of multiculturalism: dialogicalism? What happens if we see our individual identity as "not contained within us, but always . . . on the border between us and others"? (Sampson, 166). And what if, as is increasingly becoming the case, the "others" in this shared border are poor? These are American faces. They are our faces, especially the faces of the children.

Why is multiculturalism in this country having spirited conversations and confrontations across every boundary except socioeconomic class? It is not enough to say the middle class is afraid of slipping into poverty, or of their children doing so, and so they refuse to look at the injustice of the rigid class system. The occupying of a hierarchically superior position cannot be justified by saying that one fears the oppressive bottom of the economic structure. Rieff's answer to the question of why multiculturalism doesn't engage serious questions about social class is a question of his own: where does multiculturalism "fit into the material scheme of things?" (66). His unequivocal answer is that the "real ideological applications" of multiculturalism, with the collapsing of borders within the multinational corporation, result in "the multiculturalism of the market, not the multiculturalism of justice. . . . Eureka, more customers!" (70, 71).

Rieff's critique of the business of the multiculturalism industry and its economics, when added to the obvious need, because of demographic changes, for the corporation to make women and middle-class "former minorities" feel welcome, means that the "market economy, ready though it may be to admit blacks and women, is hardly likely to sign its own death warrant by accepting a radical revision of class relations" (71). These same demographic changes and resulting workforce group profiles suggest that it is in the corporation's self-interest to support the group identities (always excepting social class) that provide a motivated workforce. This "corporate multiculturalism" further suggests at least the posture by the business world, however ironic or sardonic, of an ecological-like project of preserving group diversity, the sources of its workforce. Simonson and Walker, editors of an anthology on multicultural literacy, have probably not considered the possibility of corporations co-opting the following sentiment: that as "we learn more about ecology and of ways to preserve nature, we should also learn the great value of diversity and seek to preserve a diverse cultural heritage" (xi).

There is a profound irony in contemplating the very real possibilities of American corporations of the twenty-first century celebrating "Black History Season" (three months not one), with similar merely symbolic structures for other former minorities and for women. Such an emphasis on racial, ethnic, or gender group identity in the absence of any just changes in the class structure constitutes a form of cultural imprisonment, the opposite of true multiculturalism. Thus, while purporting to support diversity (by blinking away the presence of a permanent underclass), the twenty-first century multinational will merely be insuring the continuation of the structural economic status quo of haves and have-nots; only their colors might change and their numbers increase.

While twenty-first century multinationals will be co-opting "diversity" for business motives, the democratic constitutional state will have to address the issue of survival for poor and undervalued cultural groups. Habermas has analyzed the issue of guaranteeing cultural survival. The constitutional state can try to support the continuation of all cultural groups, but it cannot guarantee survival. To do so would in effect imprison members of the group.

> When a culture has become reflexive, the only traditions and forms of life that can sustain themselves are those that bind their members while at the same time subjecting themselves to critical examination and leaving later generations the option of learning from other traditions or converting and setting out for other shores (130-31).

The true test of multiculturalism in the twenty-first century will be whether the democratic state can support the continued existence of poor and disrespected cultural groups while encouraging their economic success both by individuals leaving the cultures and by the groups as groups having real opportunities to improve their economic and political status. It should be a truism to observe that if we in the United States cannot economically grow out of poverty then there must be structural constraints on what we can do to achieve social and economic justice.

IV

> Arguments will continue to rage over how racist this society is and over the extent to which the degraded conditions experienced in American cities can be attributed ultimately to racism. But a society that will not take steps to help its poor citizens of all ethno-racial groups will have little chance to find out how successful have been its efforts to overcome the racist attitudes of empowered whites. The more inflexible the class structure, the longer will the ethno-racial groups caught in its lower segments remain there. The members of these groups will find it harder to hope for a middle-class existence and will have more and more reason to interpret as structural or institutional racism those policies that, even if devoid of prejudicial intent, have a disproportionately negative impact on them. Meanwhile, the prejudiced attitudes of some members of more prosperous groups will be reinforced by what they take to be evidence of the criminality of "other races."
>
> —David Hollinger

At the close of Ken Burns's documentary *The Civil War*, the historian Barbara Fields observes that

> what we need to remember, most of all, is that the Civil War is not over until we today have done our part in fighting it, as well as understanding what happened when the Civil War generation fought it.... If some citizens live in houses and others live on the street, the Civil War is still going on; it's still to be fought, and regrettably, it can still be lost.

In the same final segment of Burns's documentary, Fields addresses the question "who won the war?"

> If we're not talking just about the series of battles that finished up with the surrender at Appomattox but talking instead about the struggle to make something higher and better out of the country, then the question gets more complicated. The slaves won the war and they lost the war because they won freedom—that is the removal of slavery—but they did not win freedom as they understood freedom.

I see multiculturalism as the final act or process of the Civil War, and as Fields has said, this war to remake the country into something better and more democratic can be lost. If we are circumscribed by regionalism, tribalism or racism of any kind, and most especially by social class, if we cannot see that the postmodern world requires us to inhabit borders and shifting identities, we are lost. How can we multiculturally construct life and diversity, rather than the monoculturalism of death? Each of the essays in this book has addressed this question. Multiculturalism is the final battle of the Civil War because it requires the following continuing renegotiations:

1. self
2. knowledge
3. multiculturalism as a chaotic system: an ordered disorder

Self

Multiculturalism requires the letting go of the intention of complete control of the definition and sense of self. It requires acknowledgment of the permeable boundaries between self and other and, therefore, that the future is beyond our individual or primary group's control. Those with whom we enter into the substantial relationship of multicultural dialogicalism will become co-creators of our sense of self, as we will of theirs. This is not the end of self, which is after all a social construction, but instead it is the end of the illusion of complete individuality.

Knowledge

Multiculturalism opens up the white, male, hierarchical epistemology. This is the view that the expert alone has the right to speak, or at least the last word. If instead, knowledge is seen as constructed in the conversations between groups, then multicultural knowledge is fashioned around the interrogating, contesting, or perhaps sharing of what Collins calls "concrete experience as a criterion of meaning" (208; quoted in Ferber and Storrs, 38). Does not Eurocentric, masculinist epistemology see the expert as possessing his knowledge or text? Is it not better as in multiculturalism that we position ourselves as students—dialogical and open—not masters possessing knowledge or the interpretation of texts in a monological and closed system? Multiculturalism sees knowledge as a team sport and a process, not as an individual commodity loaned to us by experts, who retain ownership.

Multiculturalism as a Chaotic System: An Ordered Disorder

Multiculturalism as a chaotic system has three crucial characteristics. I will end this afterword and this book with a brief discussion of each.

Chaos is not true randomness; it is an ordered disorder. As such its complex ordering constitutes important information. Now, the peculiarity of chaos as an information system is that it is richer in information than an ordered system. Since the patterning of the strange attractors rises spontaneously out of the very chaotic process itself, negating all need for either entelechy or sheer randomicity to explain its coming-into-being, it can be said that chaos produces more meaning than it receives. It is "negentropic" in a certain sense, almost a violation of the Second Law of Thermodynamics. Likewise, multiculturalism is more than the sum of its parts. It is an open and unstable complexity that is productive of new structures and methods of adaptation which single cultures cannot achieve or construct. Multiculturalism, with its yearning for order or congruence yet its focus on unpredictability, is welcoming of the stranger within our midst, and indeed within ourselves.

What are the characteristics of multiculturalism as a chaotic system? It is excessive, violent, and creative.

Excess

The economy of multiculturalism is not one of scarcity but of excess. Multicultural language and structures are not concerned with singleness or precision of meaning, but with complexity and richness of meaning—with excess of meaning. In this sense of excess, multiculturalism resembles life itself, which is not concerned with survival only, but with expressing itself exuberantly, endlessly, expansively—a monument to excess as the key to our redemption from the myth of scarcity, penury, and limits to human growth and becoming.

I of course do not mean to disparage environmentalism here, but only that school which prescribes social poverty on the basis of an assumed scarcity somehow inherent in nature itself. Certain kinds of growth are indeed merely disguises for impoverishment—but to be truly "green" would be an expansion, not a contraction, of the human/non-human relation and its "economy."

Violence

Since multicultural language and structures seek to *break* free of monocultural codes, they necessarily commit violence. Ultimately, multicultural texts and other artifacts harbor the ambition to do violence to the order of "ordinary" monological consciousness itself: to wake one from the sleep of the quotidian, as with a Zen slapstick!—and to focus attention existentially on the real and present. This ripping open of monocultural awareness and perception constitutes one major reason for reading or writing multicultural literature and also provides an indispensable key to understanding why multicultural language does what it does. To increase the chances for a breakthrough in the reader of multicultural consciousness, writers like Rushdie use a frequent violence of imagery and metaphor, which violates rules or at least expectations about static perfection of form and "cultural purity."

Creativity

Playful or ludic awareness should not be confused with sheer frivolity. The play of children is as serious as the creativity of the artist or the visionary scientist, not the opposite of work, but something of an altogether different and higher category, akin to the Sanskrit term *lila*, the spontaneous ordering of chaos into the dance of creation. To say then that we should read multiculturalism and the texts it produces playfully is not to reduce our reading and experience to some shallow dandyism of disengaged intellect or salacious curiosity.

The play of children is not only the origin of art but also of those non-ordinary, non-monological states I have called multicultural, for surely everyone can remember, if we dare, moments in childhood when play became reverie or vision. Multicultural consciousness, which seeks congruence but is open to chaos, is a kind of human childhood or eternally present Paleolithic Age of the heart. In contact with this level of textuality, the reader becomes once more a dreamer of the dream which makes us human. To be human in this sense is not to be a disembodied brain-in-a-jar, a pair of eyes in front of a book, but rather a shape-shifter, a series of identities: thought as movement rather than stasis: "becoming" as the generosity of being rather than the entropic decay of a closed and sterile culture.

Everything is up for grabs; no one is safe, and no one can hide. But—we can invent what we want. Who do we want to be?

Works Cited

Appiah, K. Anthony. "Identity, Authenticity, Survival: Multicultural Societies and Social Reproduction." In *Multiculturalism: Examining the Politics of Recognition*. Expanded edn. by Charles Taylor, edited by Amy Guttmann. Princeton: Princeton University Press, 1994.

Arthur, John, and Amy Shapiro, eds. *Campus Wars: Multiculturalism and the Politics of Difference*. Boulder: Westview Press, 1995.

Bakhtin, Mikhail. *The Dialogical Imagination*. Edited by M. Holquist. Austin: University of Texas Press, 1986.

Calhoun, Craig, ed. *Social Theory and the Politics of Identity*. Oxford, England: Blackwell, 1994.

Collins, Patricia Hill. *Black Feminist Thought*. Boston: Unwin Hyman, 1990.

Ferber, Abby L., and Debbie Storrs. "Race and Representation: Students of Color in the Multicultural Classroom." In *Teaching a New Canon: Students, Teachers, and Texts in the College Literature Classroom*, edited by Bruce A. Goebel and James C. Hall. Urbana, IL: National Council of Teachers of English, 1995.

Folch-Serra, M. "Place, Voice, Space: Mikhail Bahktin's Dialogical Landscape." *Environment and Planning D: Society and Space* 8, (1990): 255-74.

Gitlin, Todd. *The Twilight of Common Dreams: Why America Is Wracked by Culture Wars*. New York: Metropolitan Books, 1995.

Habermas, Jurgen. "Struggles for Recognition in the Democratic Constitutional State." Trans. Shierry Weber Nicholsen. In *Multiculturalism: Examining the Politics of Recognition*. Expanded edn. by Charles Taylor, edited by Amy Guttmann. Princeton: Princeton University Press, 1994.

Hayles, N. Katherine, ed. *Chaos and Order: Complex Dynamics in Literature and Science*. Chicago: University of Chicago Press, 1991.

Hollinger, David. *Postethnic America: Beyond Multi-culturalism*. New York: Basic Books, 1995.

Hughes, Robert. *Culture of Complaint: The Fraying of America*. New York: Oxford University Press, 1993.

Johnson, Haynes. *Divided We Fall: Gambling with History in the Nineties.* New York: Norton, 1994.

Kristeva, Julia. *Strangers to Ourselves.* Trans. Leon Roudiez. New York: Columbia University Press, 1991.

Lewis, Tom J., and Robert E. Jungman, eds. *On Being Foreign: Culture Shock in Short Fiction.* Yarmouth, ME: Intercultural Press, 1986.

Rieff, David. "Multiculturalism's Silent Partner: It's the Newly Globalized Consumer Economy, Stupid." *Harper's* 287, no. 1719 (August 1993): 62-72.

Rushdie, Salman. Interview in *Newsletter on Intellectual Freedom.* 38 (1989): 106-14.

Sampson, Edward. *Celebrating the Other: A Dialogic Account of Human Nature.* Boulder: Westview Press, 1993.

Schlesinger, Arthur M., Jr. *The Disuniting of America: Reflections on a Multicultural Society.* Whittle Direct Books, 1991.

Simmel, Georg. *On Individuality and Social Forms: Selected Writings.* Edited by Donald Levine. Chicago: University of Chicago Press, [1908], 1971.

Simonson, Rick, and Scott Walker, eds. *The Graywolf Annual Five: Multicultural Literacy.* Saint Paul, MN: Graywolf Press, 1988.

Taylor, Charles. *Multiculturalism: Examining the Politics of Recognition.* Expanded edn. edited by Amy Guttmann. Princeton: Princeton University Press, 1994.

Toulmin, Stephen. *Cosmopolis: The Hidden Agenda of Modernity.* Chicago: University of Chicago Press, 1990.

Wacquant, Loic J. D. "The New Urban Color Line: The State and Fate of the Ghetto in PostFordist America." In *Social Theory and the Politics of Identity,* edited by Craig Calhoun. Oxford, England: Blackwell, 1994.

Young, Iris Marion. "Social Movements and the Politics of Difference." In *Campus Wars: Multiculturalism and the Politics of Difference,* edited by John Arthur and Amy Shapiro. Boulder: Westview Press, 1995.

Contributors

Thomas Austenfeld was born in Germany and educated at the Goerdeler-Gymnasium in Paderborn and at the University of Muenster. He holds a Ph.D. in English from the University of Virginia and serves as assistant professor of Languages and Literature at Drury College in Springfield, Missouri. He has published articles on various twentieth-century American authors and has written as well on German-American cultural relations.

Robert Eddy was educated at Boston University and the University of Nottingham, England. He holds a Ph.D. in English from the University of Durham, England. He taught at universities for three years each in England, China, and Egypt, where he was doing research and fieldwork on multicultural rhetoric. He also taught at Boston University, and he is now associate professor of English at Fayetteville State University. His book *Writing Across Cultures: A Multicultural Rhetoric* will be published by Mayfield. Mayfield will also publish his guidebook, co-authored with Victor Villanueva, on reading and writing multiculturalism. His other current book projects concern Chaos Theory and Multicultural Poetry, and a book about Malcolm X.

Dennis Fischman was educated at Yale and holds a Ph.D. in Political Science from the University of Massachusetts. He is an assistant professor of Social Sciences at Boston University. His book *Political Discourse in Exile: Karl Marx and the Jewish Question* was published by the University of Massachusetts Press in 1991. He interprets the world and tries to change it from his home in

Somerville, Massachusetts, where he is working on a book entitled *Getting It.*

Sam B. Girgus is professor of English at Vanderbilt University. He is the author of the following books: *The Films of Woody Allen, Desire and the Political Unconscious in American Literature, The New Covenant: Jewish Writers and the American Idea,* and *The Law of the Heart: Individualism and the Modern Self in American Literature.* He has also edited *The American Self: Myth, Ideology, and Popular Culture* and has edited several other books and written articles and reviews on American culture, literature, and film. He has held a Rockefeller Humanities Fellowship, a Senior Fulbright Fellowship, and has lectured at universities in many countries around the world. The subject of his essay in the current volume will be the focus of his next book.

Lloyd V. Hackley was educated at Michigan State University and holds a Ph.D. in Political Science from the University of North Carolina, Chapel Hill. He is president of the North Carolina System of Community Colleges and chairman of President Clinton's Advisory Board on Historically Black Colleges and Universities.

James Helten was educated at the University of North Dakota and holds a Ph.D. in English from that institution. He is assistant professor of English at Fayetteville State University. He has published in the area of the literature of protest.

Eric Hyman was educated at the University of California, Berkeley. He holds a Ph.D. in English from Rutgers. He is a member of the Department of English and Communication at Fayetteville State University. He has published articles on Chaucer and English linguistics.

An Lan Jang was born and educated in China, Taiwan Province, and holds an M.A. from the University of Massachusetts, Boston. Her current research is a study of the multicultural literacies in ethnic Chinese enclaves.

Solange de Azambuja Lira is a native of Rio de Janeiro, with a Ph.D. from the University of Pennsylvania in Sociolinguistics. She is an associate professor at Lesley College in Cambridge, Massachusetts, where she works with language diversity issues. She is the author of *The Subject in Brazilian Portuguese* (Peter Lang Publishing, Inc.), which won the 1994 NEMLA Prize for Best Book in language. **Arnold Gordenstein** has a Harvard Ph.D. in American Civilization, and is a professor at Fitchburg (MA) State College where he teaches American literature, minority literature, and Latin American literature. For about twelve years he taught at Federal University of Santa Catarina, in Brazil. His recently completed novel about Brazil is seeking a publisher. For more than two decades they have spent about equal amounts of time between their two countries, teaching and raising their four children, three of whom were born in Brazil. All members of the family, with varying degrees of facility, are bilingual.

Min-Zhan Lu was born and educated in China. She holds a Ph.D. in Cultural and Critical Studies from the University of Pittsburgh. She is associate professor of English at Drake University, and publishes in the areas of composition and rhetoric.

W. Maurice Shipley was educated at the University of Illinois, Urbana-Champaign and holds a Ph.D. in English from that institution. He is professor of English and Black Studies at Ohio State University. He has published in the area of Black women writers and is finishing a book on the mulatto in short prose fiction.

Victor Villanueva, Jr. was educated at the University of Washington and holds a Ph.D. from that institution. He is associate professor at Washington State University. His book *Bootstraps: From an American Academic of Color* was published in 1993 by the National Council of Teachers of English. This book has won two national awards: The David H. Russell Award from NCTE, and the Richard A. Meade Award of the Conference on English Education. Mayfield will publish his book, co-authored with Robert Eddy, called *Writing the Twenty-First Century: A Multicultural Guidebook*. He publishes in the areas of composition and literacy studies.